20
19
JOURNAL OF
POLITICAL SCIENCE

The Journal of Political Science (ISSN 0098-4612) is the official journal of the South Carolina Political Science Association and published annually by the Athenaeum Press. JoPS seeks to publish original research of high quality that contributes to all subfields of political science. We especially welcome research on Southern politics and politics on the state of South Carolina. This journal is abstracted and indexed in ProQuest and EBSCO Database Political Science Complete. Visit our website (https://digitalcommons.coastal.edu/jops/) for the online version and information on back issues.

The Athenaeum Press at Coastal Carolina University
Edwards College of Humanities and Fine Arts
P.O. Box 261954
Conway, South Carolina 29528-6054
Attn: Alli Crandell, Director

ISSN-0098-4612

The Athenaeum Press is a student-centered laboratory for design, editing, publishing, and new media
development. Located in the Thomas W. & Robin W. Edwards College of Humanities & Fine Arts
at Coastal Carolina University in Conway, South Carolina, the press uses each publication project as a
platform for enhancing undergraduate and graduate student skills across the humanities and fine arts.

COASTAL
CAROLINA
UNIVERSITY

How Prisoner Reentry Programs Influence Reentering Citizens' Trust in Government

LaTasha Chaffin DeHaan I *Elgin Community College*
Kendra Stewart I *College of Charleston*
Danielle Bloom I *College of Charleston*

This research provides insight into how reentering citizens reintegrate into society through prisoner reentry programs. Specifically, we examine the personal and economic benefits to reentering citizens and how these interventions impact their trust in government. Through a survey of participants in a South Carolina prisoner reentry program, we gained former inmates' perceptions of the programs' services on their social, economic, and political lives. We found that levels of trust in government were lower for all of the formerly incarcerated men. However, participants that were placed in governmental positions through the re-entry program recovered a substantial amount of trust in government compared to participants working in non-governmental positions or those who were unemployed.

LaTasha Chaffin DeHaan is an Assistant Professor at Elgin Community College. Kendra Stewart is a Professor of Political Science at the College of Charleston and Director of the Joseph P. Riley Jr. Center and Danielle Bloom is a graduate student at the College of Charleston. A special thank you to Amy Barch the Executive Director of Turning Leaf, Robert Kahle the Director of Research at the Riley Center for Livable Communities at the College of Charleston for his technical assistance and to the College of Charleston, Faculty Research and Development Committee for research funding support.

Introduction

The United States holds one-fourth of the world's inmates, with an incarceration rate that is unprecedented in other countries or in U.S. history (Hamilton Project A, 2016). The incarceration of inmates is costly to states and localities, with the aggregate cost in 2014 found to be $1.014 trillion dollars, which approaches 6% of GDP and is eleven times larger than corrections spending (McLauglin et al, 2016). The social and economic effects of incarceration are experienced by prisoners, their families and the community. After subtracting the value of prison production (financial savings from work performed by inmates) the average incarcerated person yielded $33,066 in lost productivity in 2014 dollars. Multiplying this productivity loss by the average jail population (744,600) yields $24.6 billion in lost wages each year (McLauglin et al, 2016).

Outside of lost wages, there are social costs to prisoners such as a sustained risk of nonfatal and fatal injuries while incarcerated, including sexual assault and suicide. Mortality rates are also higher for formerly incarcerated persons (McLauglin et al, 2016). There are disproportionate social, economic and political impacts on the incarcerated as well, especially those that are poor and minorities. Specifically, 68% of black males born after the mid-1970s that dropped out of high school have been imprisoned (Western & Pettit, 2010, Kirk & Wakefield, 2018, 176). Given the costs of incarceration and the defeating circumstances reentering citizens face, "investing in effective reentry programs may be one of the best investments we make (Petersilia, 2001)."

Often delivered by community and faith-based organizations, there are diverse reentry services to address issues facing incarcerated and released persons. Many interventions begin pre-release from prison, or reach-in services (such as the Amity In-Prison Therapeutic Community). Research surrounding pre-release programs suggests that they are most effective when paired with post-release interventions (such as Vista Aftercare Treatment), or wrap-around services (Visher et al, 2017; McCollister et al, 2003). Other organizations offer a myriad of services that individuals may use based on their needs, such as the Volunteer of America's Correctional Re-Entry Services.

While scholarship argues that it is beneficial for reentering citizens to attain meaningful employment due to the impact that social learning has on human behavior, employment alone cannot change behavior. Therefore, the attitudes and beliefs of reentering citizens should first be targeted, followed by the skills to become successful in the workforce (Latessa, 2012).

Intervention methods that may be employed generally by prison reentry programs include case management, needs assessments, reentry planning, life skills training, and employment assistance. Reentry programs are often tailored to certain populations, such as gender-specific, veterans or youth. Some programs provide issue-specific services, such as: substance abuse, mental illness, domestic violence or family-relations. They may also focus on eliminating specific barriers, for example offering housing, educational and employment opportunities.

Among the variations of programs that exist within the reentering citizen industry, this current study analyzes the Turning Leaf Project, a post-release program that assesses participants' criminogenic needs, provides case management and cognitive-behavioral therapy prior to transitioning to employment training. Specifically the study seeks to assess the effects of the Turning Leaf Project on its participants' social, economic and political lives. Turning Leaf is a prisoner reentry program that serves the greater Charleston, South Carolina area. It is a voluntary reentry program that allows rolling enrollment for formerly incarcerated, males ages 25 – 50 who are at high-risk of reoffending. The Turning Leaf Project utilizes methods grounded in evidence-based techniques that helps reduce recidivism.

First, the participants undergo a minimum of 150 hours of "classroom bootcamp" that includes concepts from cognitive behavioral therapy (CBT), individualized rehabilitation, and vocational training. Upon completing the classroom training, they transition into employment with Turning Leaf partners, which are primarily governmental entities. The cities of Charleston, SC and North Charleston, SC, along with Charleston County, are partners (along with a few private employers) in this endeavor (Turning Leaf, 2017).

The Turning Leaf program not only provides reentering citizens with opportunities to positively reshape their cognitions and identities (through CBT) and enter into a stronger labor market (through vocational training), it also provides an opportunity to address the "invisible consequences" that prisoners often face through institutional, stigmatic interactions with public entities. Specifically, reentering citizens are more likely to experience "political alienation and distrust of public authority" (Weiman et al, 2018). This research seeks to address whether prisoner reentry programs with non-paternalistic structures that also engage in government partnership, aid in recovering political trust.

Our assertion is that Turning Leaf is non-paternalistic in structure as the basis of the program is not so much to supervise these reentering citizens yet to empower them to change their lives through CBT and to make positive choices regarding whether they will complete the program. Participation in the program is voluntary and the students develop personal relationships with one another and mentor-mentee relationships with the staff at Turning Leaf and with their governmental employers. We expect that if governmental investment is made in formerly incarcerated inmates through cognitive behavioral therapy, vocational training, job acquisition and continuing support in a non-paternalistic environment then these efforts will have the effect of increasing political trust in the reentering citizen population.

Reentering Citizens
According to the Bureau of Justice Statistics, from 1990 to 2013 the population of prisoners aged 55 and older rose 234% from 43,300 to 144,500 (The Pew Charitable Trusts, 2014). Travis and Visher (2005) reported that the average age of exiting prisoners was 33 in state prisons and 37 in federal prisons (Travis and Visher, 2005, 18). In terms of gender, men have constituted the largest percentage of prisoners and parolees. However, women constitute the fastest growing percentage of the prison population (Travis and Visher, 2005, 19).

Race must also be considered in prison reentry work. Travis and Visher (2005) project that the soon-to-be released minority prison population is three times the population of minorities in the United States. Accordingly, "about one-third of soon to be released prisoners are white, 47 percent are black and 17 percent are Hispanic, who may be of any race - hence about two-thirds of all returning prisoners are racial or ethnic minorities" (Travis & Vischer, 2005, 19). For inmates in prison, Hispanics are the largest growing demographic group.

While the social, economic and political costs (with potential loss of voting rights) are high, most of the crimes are committed in a person's youth. Without early intervention, inmates have a high likelihood of recidivating as the rates of recidivism are highest in the first year after release (45%). After this, the rates fall sharply by almost 50% within the second year and almost another 50% by the third year. Persons released from prison at an older age have an even lower rate of recidivism. These results remain the same regardless of the crime type.

Furthermore, the "offender" status does not disappear after the allotted sentence has been served. While most offenders do not reoffend after their initial offence, their "offender" status can permanently hinder their opportunities for the remainder of their lives. Reentering citizens are in need of resources such as social services that provide welfare, food assistance and housing assistance along with referrals to substance abuse counseling, anger management, parenting skills and money management as well as employability skills (Andrus, 1996). A criminal record can be a significant barrier to obtaining gainful employment, restrict access to public housing, educational assistance, and income support such as Temporary Assistance for Needy Families (TANF) and Supplemental Nutrition Assistance (SNAP). In addition, legislators are continuing to restrict access to public programs for individuals with a criminal record (Hamilton Project B, 2016).

The collaboration of reach-in services (prior to release) and wrap-around services (post-release) helps improve the human capital of inmates prior to release and supports their employment and earning opportunities post-release. However, the results of studies examining whether these services have a significant impact on reducing recidivism and producing a favorable a cost-benefit analysis have been mixed (Hamilton Project B, 2016).

In 2003, the Serious and Violent Offender Reentry Initiative (SVORI), was established by the U.S. Departments of Justice Labor, Housing and Urban Development, and Health and Human Services. The program was intended to reduce recidivism, as well as to improve employment, housing, and health outcomes of participating released prisoners (Cook et al, 2014). The results, however, fell short of expectations.

In a 2012 study, the treatment effects on employment were strong during the first year, increasing the likelihood of some employment from 55.5% to 80%. Once evaluated, the increase in employment was only limited to transitional jobs and the salaries averaged at just $535 total during the first year. Employment rates during the second and third years (when transitional jobs were not offered) were unaffected. Evidence as to whether these programs work to reduce recidivism and boost long-term employment is mixed and requires more study (Cook et al, 2014, 361).

Many reentering citizens also face social and familial issues, which contributes to their unemployment. For example, financial liabilities averaging nearly $2,000, stem from a variety of sources such as: child support payments, outstanding fines and fees, court-ordered restitution payments, and other debts that the government makes efforts to collect, which put an implicit marginal tax rate on earnings (Cook et al, 2014).

Cognitive Behavioral Therapy
Cognitive-behavior therapy (CBT) has been a leading rehabilitative treatment used in prisoner reentry programs. CBT treatment interventions are those that combine elements of "behavioral modification, cognitive therapy, and social learning theory" (Sung & Gideon, 2011). Behavioralists pose that behavior is conditioned through sensory cues and consequences and cognitive theorists argue that behavior is generated by maladaptive thought patterns that derive from past experiences, and social learning theorists assert that behavior can be learned and unlearned through conditioning, modeling, and imitation.

Effectively, "cognitive-behavior therapy is based on the assumption that cognitive deficits and distortions characteristic of offenders are learned rather than inherent" (Lipsey et al, 2007). Scholarship has demonstrated that CBT has positive effects on recidivism in reentering citizens, such as up to a 25-50% decrease in the 12 months following treatment. Greater success was also associated with ex-offenders' risk level, treatment implementation, and skill components such as anger management and interpersonal problem solving (Landenberger and Lipsey, 2005; Lipsey et al, 2007).

Interventions are more likely to make an impact when they focus on areas of participants' lives that reduce risk of future criminal behavior by assessing individuals' criminogenic needs, as well as enhance quality of life. Such interventions may focus on employment, social support, and prosocial leisure habits to reduce risk behaviors (Heilbrun, Pietruszka, Thornewill, Phillips, & Schiedel, 2017).

In the current study, 80% of the Turning Leaf curriculum is grounded in CBT theory. Participants are required to complete a minimum of 150 hours of the group therapy where participants engage in role-play and modeling of how to appropriately interact with others in professional environments prior to job placement. Turning Leaf assists participants in adopting new thinking and behavior patterns which will contribute to their success in the program, in their places of employment and ultimately their lives (Turning Leaf, 2017).

Trust in Government
Hetherington (2005) defines political trust as the "degree to which people perceive that the government is producing outcomes consistent with their expectations" (Hetherington, 2005, 9). The level of trust in government depends on constituents' perceptions of the performance of government, governmental institutions and programs. Trust in government can translate into civic engagement and public support for policies that benefit minority populations such as reentering citizens (Hetherington, 2005).

Incarceration however, has been associated with declined levels of civic and institutional engagement (Kirk & Wakefield, 2018, Brayne 2014, Goffman 2014, Haskins, 2014, Lerman & Weaver 2014, Manza &Uggen 2006, Sugie 2015, Weaver et al. 2014). Scholarship has shown that individuals who have experienced authoritative, paternalistic or supervisory government programs have reduced political participation. Through direct contact with the criminal justice system, Americans' political attitudes and beliefs are shaped through the process of political socialization, or political learning, which can lead to a lack of distrust in the government and the political system (Sugie, 2015).

Weaver et al (2010) conducted a quantitative analysis using the National Longitudinal Study of Adolescent Health and the Fragile Families and Child Wellbeing Study data and found that involvement with the criminal justice system was associated with decreased trust in government, even when holding other factors constant, such as criminal behavior. Furthermore, this trust continued to decline as respondents' interactions with the criminal justice system were more severe, ranging from being questioned by the police (3% decline in trust in government), to being arrested (2%), to a court conviction (4%), to being incarcerated (9% decline in trust in government) and finally a decline in trust of 11% for those respondents that had been incarcerated for at least one year. Weaver et al. posits that this depressed trust in government causes respondents with interactions with the criminal justice system at all levels to retreat from political life, including voting and other forms of political participation. Trimbor (2009) also finds that individuals that are incarcerated have a general distrust for institutions and are skeptical about integrating into institutional networks.

White (2015) examined whether incarceration decreases voter turnout. First time misdemeanor defendant records from a Texas county were matched with their voting records and for those who received a short jail sentence, voting was decreased in the next election by several percentage points. This finding was more impactful when examined by race, as they found that despite having no demobilization effects with white defendants, black and Latino defendants experienced substantial demobilization. For Blacks that received a short jail sentence, the impact of this incarceration de-mobilized this demographic by 13 percentage points, which is substantial given that these were misdemeanor crimes, as opposed to felony crimes that could garner extensive jail or prison time. In an experiment by Gerber et al (2015), treatment groups of recently released inmates were mailed correspondence from the Connecticut Secretary of State emphasizing that they were eligible to vote, yet they were not registered. The correspondence included a voter registration card. The individuals were matched with their November 2012 voting records and it was found that this one piece of correspondence substantially reduced the 4% difference between pre-incarceration and post-incarceration voting rates. For those reentering citizens that voted in 2008, about 10% of the control group voted in 2012. However, for those that were sent the treatment letter, turnout was around 18%, or 8% higher than the control group.

Policy Feedback
According to Skocpol, policy feedback refers to the way that "policies once enacted, restructure subsequent political processes" (Skocpol, 1992, 58). Skocpol notes that new policies (and the order in which the events occur) can "affect the identities, political goals and capabilities of groups" (Skocpol, 1992, 58). It is important to assess policy feedback when considering how the public is impacted by governmental policies and programs (Skocpol; 1990, Pierson 1993; Soss & Metter 2004).

Participation in governmental programs, whether voluntary or involuntary, in the case of reentering citizens being formerly incarcerated, can assign standing or status in the political community. Beneficiaries of TANF or welfare cash assistance for example, have been branded with the stereotype of being welfare mothers, and black women of being welfare queens. Additionally, policies can establish benefits or rights and at the same time they can also establish guidelines for citizen participation, and provide implications for who is considered included in the policy, and those who are not fully included; or in other words, who are temporarily or permanently excluded or exiled. This political standing or status relates to reentering citizens who may or may not have suffrage rights depending on the state they reside in and who may have difficulty finding employment and housing because of their criminal records and who may be stigmatized as criminals even after they have paid their debt to society.

In contrast, governmental programs such as the GI bill, Title IX or Social Security Disability alternatively may provide recipients with civic teaching and knowledge about governmental processes and procedures for appealing governmental decisions and may have the effect of increasing policy beneficiaries' trust in governmental programs and institutions. However, in paternalistic programs such as TANF where recipients are heavily supervised and stigmatized, there is fear of disciplinary sanctions and recursive effects, which can cause the suppression of civic engagement and political trust (Mettler and Soss, 2004).

This paternalistic culture impacts the currently incarcerated, former felons and those who may be restricted by mandated probation and parole from voting or other forms of political participation. For reentering citizens such as the participants in the Turning Leaf program, the effects of being exiled from the polity while incarcerated and further restricted from political participation upon release can result in a suppression of civic engagement and political trust (Bruch et al, 2010; Mettler and Soss, 2004). An important aspect of reentering a democratic society is participating as a citizen in the democratic process. Research demonstrates that trust in government increases the likelihood of voting and other forms of civic engagement and therefore is an important aspect to citizen participation (Gronlund and Setala, 2007). We hypothesize that participation in a reentry program such as Turning Leaf that provides employment in the public sector will lead to participants having greater trust in government.

Data and Methods
The study included 34 males, who were formerly incarcerated and are participants of the Turning Leaf program in the Charleston, South Carolina area. The reentering participants were released and are voluntary participants of the

Turning Leaf program that provides cognitive behavioral therapy, job training, counseling, and employment outside of the judicial system.

According to the structure of the Turning Leaf program, participants are classified as Phase I or Phase II. Phase I participants undergo a minimum of 8 weeks of classroom training and move through phases of the program by reaching benchmarks and earning points for participating, being on time and showing up in their uniforms as well as turning in homework. Participants are paid a stipend to participate in the program and as they advance through the levels of Phase I their stipend increases. A few participants are engaged in temporary work in private sector jobs provided by Turning Leaf. Once a participant has earned enough points to advance from Phase I they enter into Phase II and are eligible for full-time employment provided through Turning Leaf in local government positions. Once in these positions, participants transition to working full-time during the day and receiving a paycheck from their employer while attending Turning Leaf courses during the evening. They continue to earn points through Phase II until they complete all requirements and graduate from the program. Obtaining full-time employment is the incentive to advance through the program.

Data was collected through an internet-based survey of Phase I and Phase II participants to determine the impact of the Turning Leaf program on their attitudes and behaviors, post-incarceration. While the survey was nonrandomized and the participants (all male) were known to the non-profit organization, the survey was anonymous and voided respondents' uniquely identifying information (e.g. name, address, phone number). We were unable to conduct a randomized treatment and control group to compare how the individuals within the prison reentry program fared regarding factors such as gaining employment and recovering trust in government in comparison to reentering citizens who were not participants in the program. Although an experimental model would have been preferable to tease out the causal effects of the program on the participants (Morgan and Winship, 2007), we compared Phase I participants who were required to be enrolled in the program for at least two weeks to participate in the study to Phase II participants who had undergone much of the classroom training and who had earned enough credits to be placed in employment with governmental partners. The survey was conducted by independent researchers at the College of Charleston and there was minimal compensation of $50 per participant provided by the College to participants that consented to take the survey.

The survey included approximately 60 questions, some of which were unique to each Phase I and Phase II. There were also joint questions asked of both groups. These survey questions covered a variety of important issues including participants' evaluations of the Turning Leaf program and its services, however our focus in this research is on participants' trust in government. This variable was constructed from the following survey questions: "How much of the time do you think you trust the following levels of governments to do what is right: Washington (federal government); The State Government; and the Local Government?" Response categories were "always", "most of the time", "some of the time", and "never". This variable was recoded into a dichotomy of high trust ("always" or "most of the time") and low trust ("some of the time" or "never").

To gauge how the program influenced participants' trust, we examined whether participants were employed through Turning Leaf or not. It is important to note that per the Executive Director, the structure of the program allows all participants equal opportunity to complete Phase I and receive employment. We also examined race, age, education, and their number of prison sentences. Lastly, we analyzed whether they received health and retirement benefits.

Despite having a small-n sample, this study provides insight into a national issue that our criminal justice system faces daily: how can we better reintegrate citizens back into society and ensure they participate in democratic processes?

Results

All of the participants in the Turning Leaf program have previously served either jail time or prison time. Notably, overall levels of trust in government were low for the formerly incarcerated men that participated in the Turning Leaf program. We found that participants demonstrated low trust in the following levels of government: 73% at the federal, 69% at the state and 72% at the local levels. Gallup asks these same questions of all citizens in their national poll where the numbers also demonstrate low trust in government: 48 – 56% at the federal level, 37% at the state and 28% at the local levels (Gallup, 2018). These findings were consistent with the literature suggesting that interaction with the criminal justice system (and the intensity of the interaction) yields lower trust in political institutions (Trimbor, 2009; Weaver et al, 2010).

Despite these overall low levels of trust, when we further analyzed Phase I participants compared to Phase II Turning Leaf participants, or those who had completed Phase I and had been exposed to the collaborative environment between Turning Leaf, its participants and the local city and county governments, Phase II recovered trust by substantial margins (to the degree of 20% to 40%). While these job opportunities provide economic advantages through the financial, health and retirement benefits offered, it was the opportunity for positive governmental interaction that had the greater effect of recovering trust amongst this group of reentering citizens.

The structure of the Turning Leaf program is one that is non-paternalistic, non-stigmatizing and per the participants' own voices, the program is viewed as empowering, supportive, educational, and provides equal opportunities for jobs and other resources. The following participant declarations provide evidence of how positive interactions with the program and the governments they were employed by made a significant difference in increasing reentering citizens' trust in government.

The Voices of Reentering Citizens

As members of a marginalized, often isolated community, it was important in this research to give ex-offenders and reentering citizens a voice. Regarding financial benefits of the program, some Phase I participants indicated that they were not employed through Turning Leaf yet but indicated that they were receiving a stipend from the program. Of the respondents that were employed through the program, some noted that they now have a paycheck and money in their pockets as a result of the program. Additional comments offer further insight:

- "They helped me get a great job with great benefits and taught me the social skills and thinking tools I needed to stay out of trouble, stay clean and sober and keep my job and goals successful."
- "Helping me get a job that I couldn't get on my own."
- "The pay for attending class and help us get jobs we can't normally get."
- "Paid education program [for] 8 weeks, part time job $9.00 an hr, 30 hrs a week after two weeks [un]til present and temp[orary] to perm[anent] employment with [the] City of Charleston at $11 an hour [at] 40 hours a week."
- "I was able to get a full time position with the City of Charleston, buy a car to get [to] and from work...Currently getting ready to purchase a home."

Participants were also asked about improvements to their personal relationships due to the Turning Leaf program. Responses were self-reflective and centered around participants being empowered by new learning strategies and gaining coping mechanisms that helped them to develop self-esteem, and build personal and professional relationships:

- "Improved self-respect and confidence. It has helped a whole lot"
- "It made me as a man, think before I act [and] avoid consequences"
- "I learned to interact with positive people and how to cope with stress"
- "With corrective thinking and coping strategies"
- "Turning Leaf taught me to surround myself with a better support network and social network; better people who share the same goals I share"

Lastly, when asked what could be improved about the Turning Leaf program, there were several participant comments that focused on the need for more transformative and empowering programs such as Turning Leaf, including:
- "I just wish it could be in more locations around the country to help other people all over our country and the world like it has helped me"
- "They could use help. They do a wonderful job but I would like to see them make more leaps and bounds in the[ir] journey to help ex-felons"
- "By being able to accommodate more lost souls…"

In their comments about the Turning Leaf program, reentering citizens discussed how the program was empowering and supportive, which is very different from the environments that many of these ex-offenders experienced while incarcerated. There were several comments about how the program helped participants to gain government jobs (namely at the City of Charleston) which opened the doors to financial and professional opportunities that these men would have not been exposed to, much less acquired, without the assistance of the reentry program.

Trust in Government
Turning Leaf Employment. Table 1 describes the relationship between Turning Leaf participants' employment and their reported trust in government at the federal, state, and local levels. The comparison groups represent participants who have received employment (Phase II participants) through Turning Leaf (TL) and who have not (Phase I participants). The participants employed through TL have the opportunity to work for the City of Charleston, City of North Charleston, and Charleston County. Again, "high trust" in government was indicated by reporting to trust the government "always" or "most of the time" compared to "some of the time" or "never".

Participants who were employed through Turning Leaf were more likely to report high levels of trust in government than those who were not, especially at the state and local levels. Thirty-three percent of participants employed through Turning Leaf had high trust in the federal government, compared to 17% of participants not employed through Turning Leaf. Even more notable, trust in the State Government also increased from 9% to 43%. Lastly, high trust in the Local Government increased from 9% to 38%.

Figure 1 provides a visual representation of the increase of high levels of trust in the government among participants employed through the program. When reentering citizens enrolled in the Turning Leaf program and acquired employment, they reported a 17% increase in trust in the Federal Government,

Table 1. Relationship between Trust in Government and Turning Leaf Employment

		Employed Through Turning Leaf	Not Employed Through Turning Leaf
Federal Government	HT	33%	17%
	LT	67%	83%
		100%	100%
State Government	HT	43%	9%
	LT	57%	91%
		100%	100%
Local Government	HT	38%	9%
	LT	62%	91%
		100%	100%

Notes:
[1] HT represents high trust, LT represents low trust;
[2] Column Percentages;
[3] $N = 33$.

a 34% increase in trust in the State Government, and a 29% increase in trust in the Local Government compared to those who have not received this program intervention. This data suggests that when reentering citizens progress through the program and are provided governmental jobs, they are more likely to trust the government to do what is right at all levels, but substantially at the state and local levels.

Demographics. To provide a better understanding of these findings, Table 2 displays demographic information about the participants' race, age, and highest level of education. Additionally, the number of times in prison was included in

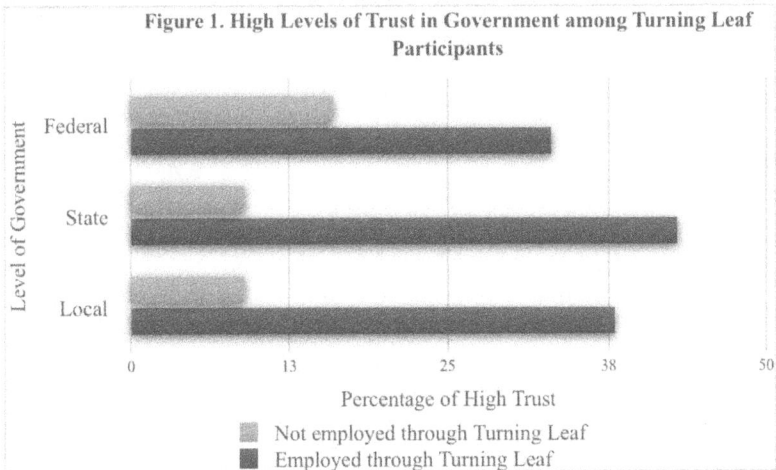

Figure 1. High Levels of Trust in Government among Turning Leaf Participants

Not employed through Turning Leaf
Employed through Turning Leaf

the demographic data as an indicator of negative interactions with government. The demographic collection was cross tabulated with the total population, employment through TL, and high trust in government to demonstrate the variation in each category.

The majority of participants were Black (85%) and the minority population was White (15%). The current data suggests that race does not explain the increased governmental trust. The demographic analysis shows that White reentering citizens' trust the government more often than Black participants; however, this gap does not explain the contrast between Turning Leaf Employment and Trust in Government provided in Figure 1 because the majority of participants employed through Turning Leaf are Black (77%).

The data in Table 2 suggests that older participants are marginally more likely to acquire Turning Leaf employment (9%) and have increased trust in government by 6%. The results indicate that age does not explain higher trust among individuals employed through Turning Leaf.

The Turning Leaf participants' education levels vary, with the majority having a high school diploma or less (76% combined). Despite this, participants with the lowest level of education (only some high school), have high rates of employment through Turning Leaf (80%). Although 100% of those with Associate Degrees

Table 2. Demographic Relationships with Turning Leaf Employment and Trust in Government

		Total	Employment Through Turning Leaf		High Trust in Government[1]		
			Yes	No	Federal	State	Local
Race	Black	85%	61%	39%	25%	30%	26%
	White	15%	80%	20%	40%	40%	40%
Age	18-24[2]	3%	–	–	–	–	–
	25-39	59%	60%	40%	25%	30%	25%
	40-59	38%	69%	31%	31%	33%	33%
Education	Some HS	30%	80%	20%	40%	40%	30%
	HS Graduate	46%	50%	50%	29%	36%	36%
	Some college	15%	60%	40%	0%	0%	0%
	Associates Degree	9%	100%	0%	33%	33%	33%
Times in Prison	Never	12.1%	50%	50%	25%	50%	50%
	1	24.2%	50%	50%	25%	25%	25%
	2-3	30.3%	70%	30%	40%	40%	30%
	4-5	9.1%	67%	33%	0%	0%	0%
	Over 5	24.2%	75%	25%	25%	29%	29%

Notes:

[1] Row percentages calculated; the remaining percentage of each subcategory reported low trust. For example, 75% of Black participants reported low trust in the federal government;

[2] Data unavailable for subgroup;

[3] $N = 33$.

secured employment through TL, the lowest education level has the next highest rate. This suggests that education does not guarantee TL employment.

Similarly, participant education and trust in government was evaluated. Although participants with some college report zero high trust in government, individuals with Associate Degrees (33%) were approximately as likely to trust the government as high school graduates (29% - 36%) and participants without a high school diploma (30% - 40%). The results indicate that education does not explain the increase in high trust in government among participants with Turning Leaf Employment.

After considering characteristics that may explain the gap between high levels of trust in those with Turning Leaf employment or without Turning Leaf employment, negative governmental interactions often have an impact on their trust. The current study utilized a survey question regarding the number of times a participant has been in prison to represent negative experiences with the government. Although responses vary, an increased return to prison does not negatively impact whether a participant receives employment provided through Turning Leaf or not. As Table 2 displays, 50% of the participants who have never been to prison attained employment, 70% of the participants who have been to prison 2-3 times gained employment, and 75% of the participants who have been to prison over 5 times received employment through Turning Leaf.

When analyzing the relationship between number of times in prison and trust in government, our data indicates similar findings. Turning Leaf participants who have been to prison once (25%) have nearly equal trust than those who have been to prison over 5 times (25% - 29%). However, as literature would suggest, those who have never been to prison trust the federal (50%) and state (50%) governments more than those who have been to prison. Interestingly, those who have been to prison over 5 times have equal trust in the federal government than those who report to have never been in prison (25%). The results suggest that the number of returns to prison does not explain the recovery of governmental trust among these reentering citizens employed in governmental positions.

Employee Benefits. Lastly, (see Table 3) displays the cross-tab relationship between employment benefits and high trust in government. The results indicate that there is an increased amount of trust among participants who receive health benefits at the state (14%) and local levels (19%).

It is important to note that retirement benefit characteristics were only collected from Phase II individuals, or those who are eligible to receive permanent employment through Turning Leaf, rather than temporary employment. We found that Phase II participants who receive retirement benefits have decreased trust in all three levels of government, however, they are more likely to trust the

Table 3: Relationship between Employee Benefits and High Trust in Government

	Health Benefits[1]		Retirement Benefits[2]		
	Yes	No	Yes	No	Unsure
Federal Government	25%	32%	23%	60%	33%
State Government	42%	28%	39%	60%	33%
Local Government	42%	23%	39%	40%	33%

Notes:

This graph only displays high trust, the remaining percentage of each subgroup reported low trust in government; therefore, columns to not equal 100%. For example, 75% of participants with health benefits reported low trust in government. Column percentages calculated.

[1] Based on $N = 33$;

[2] Phase II participants only, $N = 21$.

state and local government compared to the federal government. Those who do not receive retirement benefits have the highest level of trust, disproving that receiving retirement benefits increases trust in government. Although receiving retirement benefits is an economic advantage, it does not substantially increase participants' trust in government.

After examining the relationships between variables that may influence trust in government, employment provided by Turning Leaf was an indicator of increased trust. This was most notable in the state (43%) and local (38%) governments compared to those who were unemployed or employed without Turning Leaf employment (9%); an increase of 29%-34%. In sum, the data suggests that reentering citizens who obtain government employment after completing a reentry program are more likely to trust governmental institutions, especially at the state and local levels.

Conclusions

Previous scholarship has emphasized the importance of the government being more proactive in their efforts to re-engage ex-felons and to notify them when their voting rights have been reinstated (Gerber et al, 2015; Meredith & Morse, 2014; Porter, 2010). Most of this work has been done at the state level. However, this research brings to bear the question of whether all levels of government should consider instituting programs aimed at re-enfranchising citizens and welcoming them back into the societal family after they have paid back their debt to society through incarceration and probation or parole, if those constraints exist. Ways to do this would be through proactive efforts to encourage their civic participation (e.g. sending reentering citizens a voter registration card upon their eligibility to vote) as well as providing pathways for these citizens to re-enter the employment realm, establishing housing programs and having programs in place for the formerly incarcerated to receive psychological counseling and assistance with family reunification. Each of these intervention methods serve to reduce the societal stigma of the formerly incarcerated and to re-integrate them back into society.

We sought to determine whether prisoner reentry programs that allow for government interaction aid in recovering political trust. Studies have shown that positive experiences with government can counteract the negative experiences and recover some trust (Gerber et al, 2015). Programs such as Turning Leaf that are non-paternalistic in structure confirm prior research, as the participants in this program equally earn the opportunity to be employed through local city and county governments and have indicated positive governmental interactions. After being incarcerated and embodying overall low levels of trust in government, this positive interaction assisted this population in recovering trust to the degree of 29-34% after program participation. Participants in the Turning Leaf program have transitioned from being wards of the federal, state and local governments, to becoming public servants and trusted employees of city and county governments. These reentering citizens have come full-circle from being exiled from society to being re-integrated and accepted back into the society that expelled them.

References

Andrus, Ron. 1996. "Introduction to the Kent County Sheriff's Correctional Facility." *American Jails.* January/February.

Bahr, Stephen J., Amber S. Masters, and Bryan M. Taylor. 2012. "What Works in Substance Abuse Treatment Programs for Offenders?" *The Prison Journal* 92:155-174.

Brayne, Sarah. 2014. "Surveillance and System Avoidance Criminal Justice Contact and Institutional Attachment." *American Sociological Review* 79(3): 367-391.

Bruch, Sarah K., Myra Marx Ferree, and Joe Soss. 2010. "From Polity to Polity: Democracy, Paternalism, and the Incorporation of Disadvantaged Citizens." *American Sociological Association* 75(2): 205-226.

Cook, Philip J., Songman Kang, Anthony A. Braga, Jens Ludwig, and Mallory E. O'Brien. 2014. "An Experimental Evaluation of a Comprehensive Employment-Oriented Prisoner Re-entry Program." *Journal of Quantitative Criminology* 31(3): 355-382.

Gallup. Trust in Government. 2018. https://news.gallup.com/poll/5392/trust-government.aspx.

Gerber, Alan S., Gregory A. Huber, Marc Meredith, Daniel R. Biggers, and David J. Hendry. 2015. "Can Incarcerated Felons Be (Re)integrated into the Political System? Results from a Field Experiment." *American Journal of Political Science* 59(4): 912-926.

Gideon, Lior, and Sung Hung-En. 2011. *Rethinking Corrections: Rehabilitation, Reentry, and Reintegration.* Thousand Oaks, CA: SAGE Publications.

Goffman, Alice. 2009. "On the Run: Wanted Men in Philadelphia Ghetto." *American Sociological Review* 74(3): 339-357.

Gronlund, Kimmo, and Maija Setala. 2007. "Political Trust, Satisfaction and Voter Turnout." *Comparative European Politics* 5(4): 400-422.

Hamilton Project A. 2016. *Graduated Reintegration: Smoothing the Transition from Prison to Community.* http://www.hamiltonproject.org/papers/graduated_reintegration_smoothing_the_transition_from_prison_to_community.

Hamilton Project B. 2016. *Putting Time Limits on the Punitiveness of the Criminal Justice System.* http://www.hamiltonproject.org/assets/files/reducing_punitiveness_piehl_policymemo.pdf.

Haskins Anna. 2014. "Unintended Consequences: Effects of Paternal Incarceration on Child School Readiness and Special Education Placement." *Sociological Science* 1: 141-158.

Heilbrun, Kirk, Victoria Pietruszka, Alice Thornewill, Sarah Phillips, and Rebecca Schiedel. 2017. "Diversion at Re-entry Using Criminogenic CBT: Review and Prototypical Program Development." *Behavioral Sciences & the Law* 35(5-6): 562–572.

Hetherington, Marc. J. 2005. *Why Trust Matters: Declining Political Trust and the Demise of American Liberalism.* Princeton, NJ: Princeton University Press.

Inciardi, James A., Steven S. Martin, and Clifford. A. Butzin. 2004. "Five-Year Outcomes of Therapeutic Community Treatment of Drug-Involved Offenders after Release from Prison." *Crime & Delinquency* 50(1): 88-107.

Kirk David S., and Sara Wakefield. 2018. "Collateral Consequences of Punishment: A Critical Review and Path Forward." *Annual Review of Criminology.* 1:171-194.

James, Nathan. 2015. "Offender Reentry: Correctional Statistics, Reintegration into the Community and Recidivism." *Congressional Research Service,* https://fas.org/sgp/crs/misc/RL34287.pdf.

Landenberger, Nana A., and Mark W. Lipsey. 2005. "The Positive Effects of Cognitive-Behavioral Programs for Offenders: A Meta-Analysis of Factors Associated with Effective Treatment." *Journal of Experimental Criminology* 1(4): 451-476.

Latessa, Edward. 2012. "Why Work Is Important, and How to Improve the Effectiveness of Correctional Reentry Programs that Target Employment." *Criminology & Public Policy* 11(1): 87–91.

Laub, John H., and Robert Sampson. 2001. "Understanding desistance from crime." *Crime and Justice: An Annual Review of Research* 28:1-69.

Lee, Hedwig, Lauren Porter and Megan Comfort. 2014. "Consequences of Family Member Incarceration: Impacts on Civic Participation and Perceptions of the Legitimacy and Fairness of Government." *The Annals of the American Academy of Political and Social Science* 651(1): 44–73.

Lerman, Amy E., and Vesla M. Weaver. 2014. *Arresting Citizenship: The Democratic Consequences of American Crime Control.* Chicago: University of Chicago Press.

Lipsey, Mark W., Nana A. Landenberger, and Sandra J. Wilson. 2007. "Effects of Cognitive-Behavioral Programs for Criminal Offenders." *Campbell Systematic Reviews* 3(1): 1-27.

Listwan, Shelley, Francis Cullen, and Edward Latessa. 2006. "How to Prevent Prisoner Re-entry Programs from Failing: Insights from Evidence-based Correction." *Federal Probation* 70(3): 19-25.

Manza, Jeff, and Christopher Uggen. 2006. *Locked Out: Felon Disenfranchisement and American Democracy.* New York: Oxford University Press.

McCollister, Kathryn E., Michael T. French, Michael Prendergast, Harry Wexler, Stan Sacks, and Elizabeth Hall. 2003. "Is In-Prison Treatment Enough? A Cost-Effectiveness Analysis of Prison-Based Treatment and Aftercare Services for Substance-Abusing Offenders." *Law & Policy* 25(1): 63-82.

McLaughlin, Michael, Carrie Pettus-Davis, Derek Brown, Chris Veeh, and Tanya Renn. 2016. "The Economic Burden of Incarceration in the U.S." *Institute for Advancing Justice Research and Innovation. Washington University in St. Louis.* https://joinnia.com/wp-content/uploads/2017/02/The-Economic-Burden-of-Incarceration-in-the-US-2016.pdf.

Meredith, March, and Michael Morse. 2014. "Do Voter Rights Notification Laws Increase Ex-Felon Turnout?" *The Annals of the American Academy of Political and Social Science.* 651(1): 220-249.

Mettler, Suzanne, and Joe Soss. 2004. "The Consequences of Public Policy for Democratic Citizenship: Bridging the Policy Studies and Mass Politics." *Perspectives on Politics* 2(1): 55-73.

Mettler, Suzanne, and Mallory SoRelle. 2017. "Policy Feedback Theory." *In Theories of the Policy Process,* eds. Christopher M. Weible and Paul A. Sabatier. New York, NY: Westview Press, pp. 103-134.

Meichenbaum, Donald. 1977. *Cognitive Behavioral I Modification: An Integrative Approach.* New York: Plenum Press.

Morgan, Stephen. L., and Christopher Winship. 2007. *Counterfactuals and Causal Inference.* New York: Cambridge University Press.

Petersilia, Joan. 2001. "Prison Reentry: Public Safety and Reintegration Challenges." *The Prison Journal* 81(3): 360-375.

Pierson, Paul. 1993. "When Effect Becomes Cause: Policy Feedback and Political Change." *World Politics* 45(4): 595-628.

Porter, Nicole D. 2010. "Expanding the Vote: State Felony Disenfranchisement Reform, 1997 – 2010." *The Sentencing Project.* https://www.sentencingproject. org/wp-content/uploads/2016/01/Expanding-the-Vote-State-Felony-Disenfranchisement-Reform-1997-2010.pdf.

Ross, Robert, and Elizabeth Fabiano. 1985. *Time to Think: A Cognitive Model of Delinquency Prevention and Offender Rehabilitation.* Johnson City: Institute of Social Science and the Arts, Inc.

SCSROC. South Carolina Sentencing Reform Oversight Committee. 2015. "State Expenditures Savings Report." *State of South Carolina.* http://www. scstatehouse.gov/citizensinterestpage/SentencingReformOversightCommittee/ SROC.php.

Seiter, Richard P., and Karen R. Kadela. 2003. "Prisoner Reentry: What Works, What Does Not, and What Is Promising." *Crime & Delinquency* 49(3): 360-388.

Skocpol, Theda. 1992. *Protecting Soldiers and Mothers: The Political Origins of Social Policy in the United States.* Cambridge: Harvard University Press.

Sugie, Naomi. F. 2015. "Chilling Effects: Diminished Political Participation among Partners of Formerly Incarcerated Men." *Social Problems* 62: 550-571.

The Pew Charitable Trusts. Prison Population Continues to Age. 2014. http://www.pewtrusts.org/en/research-and-analysis/analysis/2014/10/03/ prison-population-continues-to-age.

Travis, Jeremy, and Christy Vischer. 2005. *Prisoner Reentry and Crime in America.* New York: Cambridge University Press.

Trimbur, Lucia. 2009. "Make Sense of Reentry." *Qualitative Sociology* 32(3): 259-277.

Turning Leaf. 2017. *Our Approach.* http://www.turningleafproject.org/our-approach/.

Visher, Christy, Pamela Lattimore, Kelly Barrick, and Stephen Tueller. 2017. "Evaluating the Long-Term Effects of Prisoner Reentry Services on Recidivism: What Types of Services Matter?" *Justice Quarterly* 34(1): 136-165.

Visher, Christy, and Jeremy Travis. 2003. "Transitions from Prison to Community: Understanding Individual Pathways." *Annual Review of Sociology* 29: 89-113.

Weaver, Vesla M., 2010. "Political Consequences of the Carceral State." *American Political Science Review* 104(4): 817-832.

Weaver, Vesla M., Jacob S. Hacker, and Christopher Wildeman. 2014. "Detaining Democracy? Criminal Justice and American Civil Life." *The Annals of the American Academy of Political and Social Science* 651(1): 6-21.

Weiman, David. 2007. "Barriers to Prisoners' Reentry into the Labor Market and the Social Costs of Recidivism." *Social Research* 74(2): 575-611.

Western, Bruce, and Becky Pettit. 2010. *Collateral Costs: Incarceration's Effect on Economic Mobility.* Pew Charitable Trusts. Washington, DC. http://www.pewtrusts.org/~/media/legacy/uploadedfiles/pcs_assets/2010/collateralcosts1pdf.pdf.

White, Ariel. 2015. "Misdemeanor Disenfranchisement? The Demobilizing Effects of Brief Jail Spells on Potential Voters." *Harvard Scholar.* http://scholar.harvard.edu/files/arwhite/files/misdemeanor_draft_august2015.pdf.

Wilson, David, Leana Bouffard, and Doris Mackenzie. 2005. "A Quantitative Review of Structured, Group-Oriented, Cognitive-Behavioral Programs for Offenders." *Criminal Justice and Behavior* 32(2):172-204.

Politics as Usual?
Perceptions of Political Incivility in the
United States and United Kingdom

Kylee J. Britzman | *Lewis-Clark State College*
Benjamin R. Kantack | *Georgia Gwinnett College*

Does variation in political culture affect citizens' perceptions of political incivility? We theorize that Britons, being socialized into a political culture that is more permissive of uncivil political conversation than are Americans, will therefore be less sensitive to political incivility. We test for this variation by randomly exposing Britons and Americans to video clips of either civil or uncivil televised political debates. Results provide mixed evidence that Americans tend to perceive larger differences between civil and uncivil exchanges than Britons, indicating that they are calibrated to a different range of what constitutes civil political behavior. However, although Americans' perceptions of incivility span a wider range than Britons', Americans do not perceive politics overall as being more uncivil. These findings suggest that citizens' attitudinal and behavioral responses to uncivil behavior in political campaigns may be conditioned by varying norms of political civility.

Kylee J. Britzman is an Assistant Professor at Lewis-Clark State College. Benjamin R. Kantack is an Assistant Professor at Georgia Gwinnett College

Introduction

Incivility in politics has been linked to various attitudinal and behavioral outcomes, both negative and positive (Brooks and Geer 2007; Forgette and Morris 2006; Fridkin and Kenney 2008; Maisel 2012; Mutz 2007; Mutz and Reeves 2005). Incivility's ability to both repel citizens from and attract them to the political sphere is rooted in the fact that it represents a breach of expected decorum that invites retaliation or escalation (Strachan and Wolf 2012). The extent of this breach – and, consequently, the level of preceived incivility – is heavily dependent on the decorum from which one is deviating by being uncivil.

This dependency is especially relevant in light of the fact that different scenarios abide by different standards of civility. For instance, classic work on politeness theory (Brown and Levison 1987) demonstrates that norms of politeness increase in higher-stakes situations where the potential for misunderstanding is high. This is because politeness makes communication possible when people find themselves on opposing sides of an issue, such as in formal diplomatic relations (Brown and Levison 1987). For these reasons, clearly demarcating civility from incivility is challenging, as the propriety of speech varies considerably depending on context (Maisel 2012; Muddiman 2017; Shea and Sproveri 2012; Strachan and Wolf 2012). What may be entirely appropriate in a conversation between friends may prove to be ruinously outré if uttered by a politician into a live microphone.

Just as temporal and situational variation in behavioral expectations can change the standards by which incivility is measured, societal-level differences can also affect how polite discourse is circumscribed. Civility norms, like all norms, are socially constructed (Lewis 1969; Ullmann-Margalit 1977), and therefore specifically applicable to the societies that construct them. Behavior that is considered civil in one place may seem uncivil in another place, even in scenarios that are functionally equivalent to one another but situated in different cultures (Ferree et al. 2002).

One stark demonstration of cross-national differences in what constitutes propriety is the case of politics in the United States and the United Kingdom. On the whole, British politics tends to be more uncivil than American politics. The United Kingdom's House of Commons is far more raucous than the United States' House of Representatives (Bull 2017), and congresspersons are often reprimanded for conduct that would be quotidian for Members of Parliament (Maisel 2012).[1] For example, in September 2009, Representative Joe Wilson of South Carolina, a Republican, yelled "You lie!" at President Obama during the latter's State of the Union address. After the breach of civility norms occurred,

---

[1] Jamieson (1997) notes that recent Congresses have outperformed the House of Commons on some measures of incivility, such as the prevalence of vulgarity.

members of Congress from both political parties strongly condemned the behavior, resulting in a hasty apology by Wilson (Stolberg 2009). Yet boos, shouting, heckling, and other forms of combative behavior are frequently on display in the House of Commons, especially during weekly Prime Minister's Questions sessions in the House of Commons (Allen et al. 2014). Moreover, MPs are generally rewarded rather than sanctioned for such acts (Harris 2001). British politicians also tend to be more willing than American politicians to air their disagreements on news shows, televised debates, and even comedic panel shows such as *Have I Got News for You* (Bull 2012).[2]

Although this difference between American and British political decorum has been well-documented at the elite level, its implications for mass politics have not been subject to similar scrutiny. One might expect to observe the same consequences of political incivility among Britons as have been documented among Americans, only larger, due to the higher degree of incivility. However, the incivility that characterizes British politics may also serve to normalize coarser political discourse to the point where Britons accept such dialogue as a natural aspect of politics. If Britons are socialized into a more uncivil political environment than Americans are, they may become desensitized to rhetoric that Americans would regard as a violation of political propriety. Furthermore, they may be inoculated against the attitudinal and behavioral effects of political incivility to which Americans are subject.

We theorize that socialization into British and American political culture imparts to citizens norms of civility that condition their sensitivity to incivility in the political sphere. Accordingly, we hypothesize that Britons, being calibrated to a higher tolerance of coarse political discourse than Americans, will be less sensitive to political insensitivity than Americans.

Research Design
We recruited 253 Britons and 235 Americans via the online crowdsourcing platforms Amazon Mechanical Turk and Prolific in March 2017.[3] Platforms such as these can match or exceed convenience samples in terms of data quality (Berinsky, Huber, and Lenz 2012; Buhrmester, Kwang, and Gosling 2011; Hauser and Schwarz 2016; Paolacci, Chandler, and Ipeirotis 2010) while being more economical than a nationally-representative survey. In terms of

[2] Beyond politics, British reality television is also more impolite and blunter than its American counterpart. For example, the sardonic Simon Cowell has a reputation for meanness in the United States, but his acerbic mockery stands out much less in the United Kingdom (Culpeper and Holmes 2013).

[3] Replication data for this study are available from the authors upon request.

demography, our British and American samples were not substantially different, apart from nationality.[4]

Each subject viewed four video clips (each lasting 75 to 80 seconds), one from each of four political debates – a 2016 Australian debate between prime ministerial candidates Bill Shorten and Malcolm Turnbull, a 2016 Canadian debate between Saskatchewan premier candidates Cam Broten and Brad Wall, a 2016 British debate between London mayoral candidates Zac Goldsmith and Sadiq Khan, and a 2015 American debate between Louisiana gubernatorial candidates John Bel Edwards and David Vitter. We specifically chose debates between male candidates to avoid inducing any gender bias that may exist in perceptions of political incivility. We used debates from Australia and Canada to serve as "neutral sites" in case Britons or Americans, perhaps detecting familiar accents or recognizing the debaters, would be biased in their evaluations of incivility among their own countrymen.

Incivility was operationalized not by the content of what the candidates said but rather their behavior toward one another.[5] This operationalization is similar to that of Coe, Kenski, and Rains (2014), who argue that incivility refers to "features of discussion that convey an unnecessarily disrespectful tone toward the discussion forum, its participants, or its topics" (660). Examples of incivility within the debate clips included frequent interruptions, raised voices, harsh speaking tones, adversarial body language, and dismissive comments directed toward one's opponent.[6] By selecting debates from campaigns for subnational offices (with the exception of the Australian prime ministerial debate), we endeavored to make sure the content of the discussion would be unfamiliar to most subjects.[7] This was done to encourage subjects to focus not on the content of the debate but on the civil or uncivil manner in which the content was delivered.

---

[4] Our British and American samples were similar on a variety of characteristics, including percent female (60.5% versus 54.9%, respectively), mean age (36.5 versus 40.9), percent white (87.4% versus 78.3%), possession of a college degree (49.4% versus 56.2%), and median income range (£30,000-£39,999 versus $40,000-$49,999). On a left-right ideological scale ranging from 1 to 10, the mean self-placement was 4.4 for Britons and 4.9 for Americans.

[5] An alternative operationalization of incivility would be one based on the content of the debate, such as whether the debaters invoked sexist or racist terminology or engaged in explicitly personal attacks. For the purposes of this study, we chose to focus our attention on incivility of style rather than incivility of content.

[6] Full transcripts of the debate clips are included in Appendix B.

[7] Examples of the topics discussed in the debates include taxes, transportation, incentives for businesses, and college tuition costs.

Based on random assignment to one of four treatment conditions, each subject viewed either one civil clip or one uncivil clip from each debate in random order. This allowed us to keep the candidates and debates constant across all treatments, such that the only variation was the level of incivility in the clips. Roughly one quarter of subjects viewed four civil clips while another quarter viewed four uncivil clips, with the remaining subjects viewing one of two combinations of two civil and two uncivil clips.[8]

After watching each clip, subjects were immediately asked to rate the two candidates featured in the clip on five seven-point scales whose endpoints were labeled with trait pairs (emotional/unemotional, quarrelsome/cooperative, hostile/friendly, rude/polite, agitated/calm) before proceeding to the next clip.[9] We averaged these ratings for each candidate and rescaled each average from 0 to 1, such that 0 and 1 indicated the least and most uncivil ratings possible, respectively.

Results

To assess how subjects responded to candidate incivility, we estimated eight ordinary least squares regressions, one for each candidate. For each model, the dependent variable was a candidate-specific incivility rating calculated by averaging the five trait measures. Treatments were collapsed into two groups depending on whether subjects viewed the candidate in question in a civil or uncivil clip. These uncivil treatment variables were interacted with an indicator variable coded as 0 for Britons and 1 for Americans, allowing us to estimate variations in treatment effects by subjects' nationality.

Table 1 displays the results of these models. For six of the eight candidates (Shorten, Broten, Goldsmith, Khan, Edwards, and Vitter), the difference between subjects' incivility ratings or the civil and uncivil clip was statistically significant ($p < .05$) and in the expected direction – candidates in uncivil clips were rated as more uncivil than the civil treatment. The exceptions were Wall, whom subjects rated as being similarly uncivil regardless of treatment, and Turnbull, who was rated as being more uncivil in the civil treatment than in

---

[8] In one "mixed" condition, the Australian and Canadian clips were civil and the British and American clips were uncivil. In the other mixed condition, the Australian and Canadian clips were uncivil and the British and American clips were civil.

[9] These trait pairs were taken from Mutz and Reeves (2005). See Appendix A for specific question wording. We chose the rating measures to replicate prior work on political incivility and to leverage a multi-item measure of incivility.

the uncivil treatment.[10] These findings generally comport with our expectation that subjects would concur with our prior judgments about the relative civility of the clips.

Table 1. Effects of Uncivil Treatment and Nationality on Candidate Incivility Ratings

Variable	Australia		Canada		United Kingdom		United States	
	Shorten	Turnbull	Broten	Wall	Goldsmith	Khan	Edwards	Vitter
Uncivil Treatment	0.061**	−0.042**	0.161***	0.041	0.050**	0.064**	0.051*	0.054**
	(0.020)	(0.019)	(0.021)	(0.024)	(0.021)	(0.021)	(0.020)	(0.021)
American	−0.051*	−0.103***	−0.033	−0.036	0.027	0.051*	−0.040	−0.035
	(0.021)	(0.019)	(0.022)	(0.024)	(0.021)	(0.022)	(0.021)	(0.021)
Uncivil Treatment × American	−0.001	0.126***	0.082**	0.004	−0.043	−0.020	0.072*	0.071*
	(0.029)	(0.027)	(0.030)	(0.034)	(0.030)	(0.030)	(0.030)	(0.030)
Constant	0.483***	0.545***	0.549***	0.521***	0.484***	0.453***	0.493***	0.521***
	(0.015)	(0.014)	(0.016)	(0.018)	(0.015)	(0.015)	(0.015)	(0.015)
N	488	488	488	488	488	488	488	488
R^2	0.06	0.06	0.27	0.02	0.01	0.04	0.08	0.08

Notes:
[1] Dependent variable: Candidate incivility rating
[2] Standard errors in parentheses
[3] Significance levels: * : 5% ** : 1% *** : 0.1%

In terms of our expectation that Americans would adjust their ratings more drastically when exposed to incivility, we find mixed support. The interaction coefficient was significant and positive for four candidates (Turnbull, Broten, Edwards, and Vitter), and insignificant for the remaining four (Shorten, Wall, Goldsmith, and Khan).[11] These significant positive interaction coefficients indicate that the effect of the uncivil treatment was larger for American subjects than for British subjects, consistent with our expectation that Americans would exhibit greater sensitivity to political incivility. Figure 1 displays predicted probabilities based on these models.

Notably, Americans' incivility ratings are not uniformly higher than Britons' incivility ratings. Indeed, the coefficient for American nationality was significant and positive for only one of the eight candidates (Khan). This absence of an independent nationality effect suggests that the difference between British and

[10] We suspect this is because Wall and Turnbull were especially dominated by their opponents and moderators in the uncivil treatments in terms of speaking time and volume, reducing subjects' exposure to them and possibly lowering their incivility ratings as a result. See Appendix B for evidence of this domination in the debate transcripts.

[11] The absence of a significant interaction effect for either Goldsmith or Khan may be partially attributable to the salience of those candidates among our British subjects, who may have recalled the bitterness of the 2016 London mayoral campaign when viewing the uncivil treatment (Booth and Asthana 2016).

Figure 1: Predicted Incivility Ratings by Treatment and Subject Nationality
(with 95% Confidence Intervals)

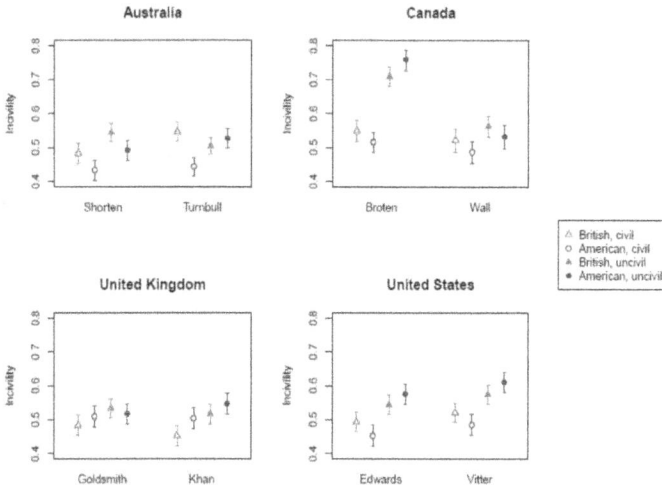

American perceptions of incivility is a matter not of baseline but rather of range.[12] Britons, socialized into a political culture that is much more accommodating of roughness in political discussion, are calibrated to a wider range of incivility, and consequently less prone to providing extreme incivility ratings than their counterparts across the pond.

The heterogeneity of treatment effects across the four debates and eight debaters suggests that subjects may be responding not to incivility as a generalized construct but to specific behaviors. Although we are relatively confident in claiming that each "civil" debate clip was more civil than the "uncivil" clip from the same debate, the types of incivility on display varied considerably among debates and debaters.[13] With few clips and many differences among them, we are unable to isolate the individual effects of interruptions, raised voices, name-calling, accusations of falsehood, or other specific behaviors on perceptions of

---

[12] It is possible that we would have observed an independent nationality effect had we anchored subjects' incivility judgments prior to the experiment, perhaps by showing two additional clips and providing an objective classification of them according to our incivility scales. Instead, we left the interpretation of our incivility scales entirely up to the subjects.

[13] For example, Shorten never interrupted his opponent in the uncivil Australian clip, whereas Broten and Wall interrupted each other constantly in the uncivil Canadian clip. Similarly, Broten and Wall, along with Edwards, raised their voices markedly in their respective uncivil clips, while Goldsmith and Khan kept theirs relatively low during their uncivil clip.

incivility. Rather than attempt a post-hoc rationalization of our mixed results, we merely acknowledge the possibility that Americans may be picking up on particular behaviors as evidence of incivility that Britons are less likely to flag as breaches of decorum.

Conclusion

The power of incivility to influence citizens' political perceptions and behaviors stems from its transgressive quality. As such, incivility can only be defined with respect to boundaries that circumscribe appropriate conduct for particular circumstances. Because these boundaries vary from circumstance to circumstance, behavior which is acceptable (and unremarkable) in one scenario may be unacceptable (and inflammatory or upsetting) in another.

We find qualified support for the theory that transatlantic differences in civility norms contribute to differences between British and American perceptions of incivility in politics. Compared to Britons, Americans tend to be more sensitive to variation in the incivility of politicians' behavior during televised debates, though they do not appear to rate all political discussion as being intrinsically more uncivil. Put another way, Americans see larger differences between civil and uncivil behavior but do not necessarily have a different threshold than Britons for what constitutes incivility in politics. This heterogeneity mirrors the distinction between British and American political cultures, the former of which is considerably more permissive of coarse and confrontational discourse.

Our conclusions underscore the importance of being mindful of contextual differences when analyzing political phenomena. Exposure to political disagreement and incivility has been found to have a demobilizing and disengaging effect on political participation in the United States (Mutz 2002; Mutz and Reeves 2005), and a mobilizing and engaging effect on political participation in the United Kingdom (Pattie and Johnston 2009). What may at face value appear to be contradictory findings can be easily reconciled if Britons are more inured to incivility in politics – and therefore less put-off when they encounter it – as a consequence of their being socialized into a political culture that tolerates a wider range of uncivil behavior.

Our study is limited to establishing that variation exists between British and American perceptions of political incivility. Future research would do well to explore the attitudinal and behavioral consequences of this variation, such as whether incivility norms moderate the effects of exposure to disagreement on political trust, political efficacy, and willingness to participate in politics. Another potential line of inquiry would be to decompose political incivility into its constituent parts to determine what if any individual components of political incivility (insults, vulgarity, raised voices, interruptions, etc.) account for British insensitivity and American sensitivity to incivility.[14] Our experimental treatments do not permit us to disaggregate incivility in this way, but we acknowledge that what we identify as responsiveness to overall incivility may in fact be primarily driven by one or two particular types of uncivil behavior.

In contemporary politics, many Americans lament a decline in political civility that is begetting rougher political discourse (Scott 2017). Incivility can motivate people to become more interested in and increasingly engage with politics, but incivility and calls for increased civility can also marginalize or silence underrepresented groups in society (Jamieson et al. 2017). Determining whether a civil or uncivil political culture is "better" for the health of a democracy and identifying the potential short- and long-term consequences of each is difficult. However, if our theory of sensitivity to incivility correctly characterizes British and American political cultures, the specter of uncivil politics may bear the silver lining of socializing the next generation of American citizens to be less affected by transgressive political talk. Only time will tell whether Americans in the future will more resemble their British counterparts in terms of their desensitization to political incivility – and, if so, whether American politics will be better for the evolution.

---

[14] This could be done through fictional debates in the style of Mutz and Reeves (2005), which would allow variation in individual behaviors while keeping others constant. Another fruitful avenue might be to explicitly ask Britons and Americans to rate specific behaviors based on how uncivil they perceive them to be in the realm of politics.

References

Allen, Beccy, Ruth Fox, Isla Geis-King, Virginia Gibbons, Matt Korris, Petya Pavlova, and Michael Raftery. 2014. "Tuned In or Turned Off? Public Attitudes to Prime Minister's Questions." *Hansard Society.* http://doc.ukdataservice.ac.uk/doc/7577/mrdoc/pdf/7577_tuned_in_or_turned_off_public_attitudes_to_pmqs_2014.pdf.

Berinsky, Adam J., Gregory A. Huber, and Gabriel S. Lenz. 2012. "Evaluating Online Labor Markets for Experimental Research: Amazon.com's Mechanical Turk." *Political Analysis* 20(3): 351-368.

Booth, Robert, and Anushka Asthana. 2016. "Sadiq Khan Easily Beats Zac Goldsmith to Become London Mayor." *The Guardian* May 6.

Brooks, Deborah Jordan, and John G. Geer. 2007. "Beyond Negativity: The Effects of Incivility on the Electorate." *American Journal of Political Science* 51(1): 1-16.

Brown, Penelope, and Stephen C. Levinson. 1987. *Politeness: Some Universals in Language Usage.* Cambridge: Cambridge University Press.

Buhrmester, Michael, Tracy Kwang, and Samuel D. Gosling. 2011. "Amazon's Mechanical Turk: A New Source of Inexpensive, Yet High-Quality, Data?" *Perspectives on Psychological Science* 6(1): 3-5.

Bull, Peter. 2012. "Adversarialism in British Political Interviews." In *L'Échange Politique la Télévision: Interviews, Débats et Divertissements Politiques,* eds. Patrick Amey and Pierre Leroux. Paris: L'Harmattan.

Bull, Peter. 2017. "Civility and Incivility at Prime Minister's Questions (PMQ) in the British House of Commons." Presented at the European Consortium for Political Research Joint Sessions, Nottingham, UK, April 25.

Coe, Kevin, Kate Kenski, and Stephen A. Rains. 2014. "Online and Uncivil? Patterns and Determinants of Incivility in Newspaper Website Comments." *Journal of Communication* 64(4): 658-679.

Culpeper, Jonathan, and Oliver Holmes. 2013. "(Im)politeness and Exploitive TV in Britain and North America: *The X Factor* and *American Idol.*" In *Real Talk: Reality Television and Discourse Analysis in Action,* eds. Nuria Lorenzo-Dus and Pilar Garcés-Conejos Blitvich. New York: Palgrave MacMillan.

Ferree, Myra Marx, William A. Gamson, Jürgen Gerhards, and Dieter Rucht. 2002. "Four Models of the Public Sphere in Modern Democracy." *Theory and Society* 31(3): 289-324.

Fishkin, James S. 1991. *Democracy and Deliberation: New Directions for Democratic Reform.* New Haven: Yale University Press.

Forgette, Richard, and Jonathan S. Morris. 2006. "High Conflict Television News and Public Opinion." *Political Research Quarterly* 59(3): 447-456.

Fridkin, Kim L., and Patrick J. Kenney. 2008. "The Dimensions of Negative Messages." *American Politics Research* 36(5): 694-723.

Hauser, David J., and Norbert Schwarz. 2016. "Attentive Turkers: MTurk Participants Perform Better on Attention Checks Than Do Subject Pool Participants." *Behavioral Research Methods* 48(1): 400-407.

Herbst, Susan. 2010. *Rude Democracy: Civility and Incivility in American Politics.* Philadelphia: Temple University Press.

Harris, Sandra. 2001. "Being Politically Impolite: Extending Politeness Theory to Adversarial Political Discourse." *Discourse & Society* 12(4): 451-472.

Jamieson, Kathleen Hall. 1997. "Civility in the House of Representatives." *Annenberg Public Policy Center Report #10* http://www.annenbergpublicpolicycenter.org/civility-in-the-house-of-representatives/.

Jamieson, Kathleen Hall, Allyson Volinsky, Ilana Weitz and Kate Kenski. 2017. "The Political Uses and Abuses of Civility and Incivility." In *The Oxford Handbook of Political Communication,* eds. Kate Kenski and Kathleen Hall Jamieson. Oxford: Oxford University Press.

Lewis, David. 1969. *Convention: A Philosophical Study.* Cambridge: Harvard University Press.

Maisel, L. Sandy. 2012. "The Negative Consequences of Uncivil Political Discourse." *PS: Political Science & Politics* 45(3): 405-411.

McClurg, Scott D. 2006. "The Electoral Relevance of Political Talk: Examining Disagreement and Expertise Effects in Social Networks on Political Participation." *American Journal of Political Science* 50(3): 737-754.

Muddiman, Ashley. 2017. "Personal and Public Levels of Political Incivility." *International Journal of Communication* 11: 3182-3202.

Mutz, Diana C. 2002. "The Consequences of Cross-Cutting Networks for Political Participation." *American Journal of Political Science* 46(4): 838-855.

Mutz, Diana C. 2006. *Hearing the Other Side.* New York: Cambridge University Press

Mutz, Diana C. 2007. "Effects of 'In-Your-Face' Television Discourse on Perceptions of a Legitimate Opposition." *American Political Science Review* 101(4): 621-635.

Mutz, Diana C., and Byron Reeves. 2005. "The New Videomalaise: Effects of Televised Incivility on Political Trust." *American Political Science Review* 99(1): 1-15.

Paolacci, Gabriele, Jesse Chandler, and Panagiotis G. Ipeirotis. 2010. "Running Experiments on Amazon Mechanical Turk." *Judgment and Decision Making* 5(5): 411-419.

Pattie, Charles J., and Ronald J. Johnston. 2009. "Conversation, Disagreement, and Political Participation." *Political Behavior* 31(2): 261-285.

Scott, Eugene. 2017. "Poll: Majority of Americans Say Civility Has Declined Since Trump Elected." CNN. July 3. http://www.cnn.com/2017/07/03/politics/npr-poll-trump-civility-declined/.

Shea, Daniel M., and Alex Sproveri. 2012. "The Rise and Fall of Nasty Politics in America." *PS: Political Science & Politics,* 45(3): 416-421.

Strachan, J. Cherie, and Michael R. Wolf. 2012. "Political Civility: Introduction to Political Civility." *PS: Political Science & Politics,* 45(3): 401-404.

Stolberg, Sheryl Gay. 2009. "Obama Accepts Wilson's Apology." *New York Times* September 10.

Ullmann-Margalit, Edna. 1977. *The Emergence of Norms.* Oxford: Clarendon Press.

Uslaner, Eric M. 1993. *The Decline of Comity in Congress.* Ann Arbor: University of Michigan Press.

Wolf, Michael R., J. Cherie Strachan, and Daniel M. Shea. 2012. "Incivility and Standing Firm: A Second Layer of Partisan Division." *PS: Political Science & Politics,* 45(3): 428-434.

Appendix A: Civility Ratings

Based on what you saw, how would you describe [CANDIDATE]? Using the word pairs below, please click the circle that best describes him.

Emotional o o o o o o o Unemotional

Quarrelsome o o o o o o o Cooperative

Friendly o o o o o o o Hostile

Rude o o o o o o o Polite

Calm o o o o o o o Agitated

Appendix B: Debate Clip Transcripts

Australia, Civil

Turnbull: ...the other thing, and you'd see this in Gilmore, if you're living down the south coast, there are so many people there that are benefitting from the big trade export markets we've opened up. Now those achievements – those agreements – were executed, were agreed, during our term of government just over the last three years. And what they're doing is driving stronger growth in regional Australia. And you're seeing that benefiting farmers, you're seeing that food processors, tourism in particular is benefitting enormously. So we're putting more – there is more growth and more jobs in regional Australia, and that is because our national economic plan is working.

Moderator: Mr. Shorten, what's Labour's jobs plan? We haven't really heard much of one, have we?

Shorten: Oh, yes we have, but – we've been talking about it for the last week and a half, Joe. But I'm happy to talk about Gilmore and Nowra and Ulladulla and other great places to live. I don't want to see young people having to leave their country towns to be able to pursue their futures, without at least having choices to be able to do so locally. So our plan for jobs is to make sure that we've got a good education system. Give a child a good education system and you'll set them up for life. I've been very disturbed that, under the Liberal administration the last three years, that we've fallen from 415,000 apprenticeships down to 295,000...

Australia, Uncivil

Turnbull: I don't think it's the government's role to be telling the Fair Work Commission what to do about penalty rates. It's meant to be an independent – it's meant to be independent of government. And, can I – you know, you've got to recognize, when you're running the AWU, you negotiated deals for – on behalf of your members with employers to vary penalty rates. Often they are varied between the union and the employer, and that's part of an open negotiation. But, as far as the awards, which cover everyone subject to those agreements, that's a matter for the independent umpire. And we believe the independent umpire should be independent and not be leant on by government one way or the other.

Shorten: Mr. Turnbull says he respects the independent umpire. There was something called the Road Safety Remuneration Tribunal. That was the independent umpire setting rates for owner drivers. He

	got rid of it. So when he didn't like what they did, he didn't just put in a submission. He nuked it!
Turnbull:	Well, that's a good –
Moderator:	So, if you could –
Turnbull:	We should –
Moderator:	One second, please –
Turnbull:	We should, we should talk about –
Moderator:	So, Mr. Shorten, so –
Turnbull:	That's a good issue.
Moderator:	– would you respect the independent umpire? If Fair Work Australia says yes, we've actually decided there is a case for reducing Sunday penalty rates to Saturday levels, for example, which is one option they've talked about – you respect the umpire's decision, you'll cop that?
Shorten:	It's not going to happen, because I've had a look at the evidence. It's five –
Turnbull:	Hmph.
Shorten:	Well, I've actually read the submissions, Malcolm, and you've said it's none of your business so you wouldn't have – I've read the submissions and I've looked at the evidence…

Canada, Civil

Wall:	…and that's what we have today in Saskatchewan. Under Creative Saskatchewan, we're providing grants to film. That's why *Corner Gas* was made here. That's why *WolfCop 1* and *2* were made here. Now, the Province of Alberta has a grant program. Their – the budget for the grants are much more significant, certainly. We readily agree with that. But we also believe it's important for us to invest in the other arts genres – in music, in visual arts, in live drama. And that's what Creative Saskatchewan's been tasked to do. And so I think it's very important that we have balance with respect to funding, for all of the arts.
Moderator:	And keep in mind, just so you know at home, it's 30 seconds for the rebuttal answers. Tough to do, I understand that, and I respect it, but we're doing very well. 30 seconds to you, Mr. Broten, on this matter.

Broten: Mr. Wall's refusal to admit that it was a massive mistake to kill the film employment tax credit is just proof that he's not listening. Proof that they've dug in their heels, and they're very stubborn, this Sask Party government. Everyone in the province knows that the film industry not only made us proud as Saskatchewan people, but it made us millions. Even the provincial chamber of commerce said that for a one million dollar expense it actually brought 45 million dollars of revenue into the province each year. Yes, we need to support all film – all creative industries, but we need to have a film employment tax credit once again here in Saskatchewan.

Canada, Uncivil

Broten: You, once upon a time, talked about how it was an advantage to be part of an administration that lost its way. But we see the exact thing – same thing happening here right now –

Wall: Oh, this is just nonsense. Mr. Broten, this is nonsense –

Broten: Why was one parcel of land treated differently –

Wall: There was an appraisal –

Broten: – than all of the other areas?

Wall: There was an appraisal from the seller –

Broten: And where is that appraisal?

Wall: There was an appraisal from the government –

Broten: You just denied the Freedom of Information request, didn't you?

Wall: It's a hundred and twenty-nine thousand dollars. The GTH –

Broten: You just – that's service land. You know that.

Moderator: One at a time, one at a time.

Wall: The GTH denied –

Broten: That's service land. You know that.

Wall: The GTH denied the request – I'm asking the GTH –

Broten: We're talking about raw farmland.

Wall: – to contact the appraiser and authorize its release –

Broten: Oh, pfft!

Wall: – because the release of that appraisal –

Broten: You know, Mr. Wall –

Wall:	– will show 129,000. We bought it for 103,000 –
Broten:	We're talking about service land versus other land.
Wall:	– and guess what? 30 acres of GTH land –
Broten:	I've stood in that field!
Wall:	– is selling for 250,000! Taxpayers are making money on that –
Broten:	If you try to claim right now –
Wall:	Taxpayers are making money –
Broten:	– that taxpayers made a deal –
Wall:	250,000 dollars an acre –
Broten:	– you are more stubborn –
Wall:	It's exactly what we got a couple weeks ago –
Broten:	– and not listening like I've never seen before, Mr. Wall.
Wall:	– for 30 acres. We paid a hundred and three –
Broten:	No one in Saskatchewan thinks that's true!
Wall:	– they're selling for two hundred fifty.
Broten:	Only you, and Bill Boyd, and the businessmen who made millions off of it.
Wall:	I like how you resist hyperbole.
Broten:	You allowed the nuns to get ripped off –
Wall:	"No one in Saskatchewan" –
Broten:	– which is the gospel truth.
Wall:	Oh, Mr. Broten –
Broten:	You allowed the nuns to get ripped off –
Wall:	Mr. Broten –
Broten:	– you allowed land to be flipped numerous times –
Wall:	You know –
Moderator:	We have five seconds.
Broten:	– and it's your signature on the bottom of the document. You authorized that sale.
Wall:	I understand it –
Moderator:	Okay –

Broten:	You authorized it.
Wall:	I understand why you're grandstanding –
Broten:	You don't understand.
Wall:	– I understand the hyperbole –
Moderator:	We –
Wall:	– you're desperate. It's a desperate season for you politically –
Moderator:	We have to leave it at that. Sorry, gentlemen.
Broten:	That's cocky.
Moderator:	I tell you what, we are –
Broten:	That's a real big arrogance. That's another one of your changes –
Moderator:	Excuse me, we're running out of time…

United Kingdom, Civil

Moderator:	Is this going to be a dirty campaign? You've called Zac a "serial underachiever."
Khan:	I think it's really important that Londoners compare or contrast our respective CVs. What I think is not helpful is if you try and divide communities, or we try and talk about background. I will never talk about Zac's background. What is relevant to talk about is what we've done since we've been adults, whether that's businesses we've run successfully, whether we've served in government, whether we've made tough decisions, whether we've made balance sheets balance. And I think those are really important for Londoners to know about.
Moderator:	Okay, fine. He says he's not going to talk about your personal background, but he's just suggested you don't have the CV for it.
Goldsmith:	If you look at my record as an MP – it's very odd that Sadiq Khan doesn't seem to regard being an MP as a job. Maybe that's why he's managed to turn a safe Labour seat into a marginal. You look at my record as an MP, where I took on a Lib Dem seat, a comfortable Lib Dem seat, and got the biggest swing of any MP in the country. The people who know me best, who saw me in action, knew that I was on their side. I was elected to take a stand against Heathrow expansion. I won that campaign. I was elected to protect funding for Kew Gardens. I protected funding for Kew Gardens. I got a string of successes that my constituents prized greatly, and as a

consequence people who'd never voted Conservative before voted Conservative for the first time –

Moderator: You talk about winning Heathrow. It's not over yet.

Goldsmith: I disagree with you. Heathrow is now being required to pass a pollution test which you and I know it can never pass...

United Kingdom, Uncivil

Khan: ...we can cut down on fare evasion. Last year it cost us 61 billion pounds –

Moderator: Don't you think Transport for London are trying to do that anyway?

Khan: No, because you've had a – as the viewer said, we've had a part-time mayor more interested in his next job –

Moderator: – he's got to take –

Khan: – than in actually taking charge –

Moderator: Transport for London is presumably –

Khan: We have a huge –

Goldsmith: If I could just make one correction –

Khan: Why don't we keep hold of the freehold of TFL, build these homes that we need, and have a revenue stream come in? You know, Hong Kong's transport authority raises more money via clever use of its property than by fares. What we need is a full-time mayor –

Moderator: So –

Khan: – committed to use the experience he has as a Transport Minister –

Goldsmith: Transport for London –

Khan: – and making tough decisions with a successful business to make sure TFL works for Londoners.

Goldsmith: Transport for London –

Moderator: If you disagree with Transport for London's figure of 1.9 billion as the cost –

Khan: It's not their figure!

Goldsmith: It is their figure.

Khan: It's not.

Goldsmith: Transport for London have taken the unprecedented step of correcting Sadiq Khan's figures, pointing out that they're out by about 400%. Tony Travers, who Sadiq Khan has just quoted, has said yes you could take two billion pounds out of the budget, but it would be undesirable –

Khan: Oof.

Goldsmith: – because it would freeze the expansion program that London is –

Khan: That's not true.

Goldsmith: What Sadiq Khan needs to do –

Khan: Desperate, Zac –

Goldsmith: – is explain which of the programs he's going to cut. Is it the night tube? Is it the Freedom Pass? Is it the Circle Line upgrades?

Khan: This is desperate stuff, Zac, this is desperate stuff.

Goldsmith: The District Line upgrades? You cannot take two billion pounds –

Khan: Ugh.

Goldsmith: – out of the budget –

Khan: Ugh.

Goldsmith: Find me an independent –

Khan: Ugh.

Goldsmith: – expert who believes you can do what you say you're going to do without decimating the program –

Khan: If I've got some time to respond to, desperate stuff –

Goldsmith: – and I think you need to be honest with voters. What are you going to cut?

United States, Civil

Edwards: ...we will double the Port Priority program overnight. Now, clearly, the single biggest road infrastructure improvement that we need in Louisiana is the I-10 corridor through Baton Rouge. I am committed to working on that project first, but it is not like that's the only pressing priority. We have I-49 South from Lafayette, I-49 North in Shreveport, we have off-ramps that are needed on 10 in New Orleans to the airport – all of these things are priorities. But they're all going to require a strategic plan to get the money necessary to address those needs, because it's inhibiting – first of all, it's a quality of life issue if you're hung up in traffic, but it's

	inhibiting commerce and economic development and job creation as well.
Moderator:	Thank you, sir. Same question to you, Senator Vitter –
Vitter:	Jeff –
Moderator:	Can you identify three –
Vitter:	Sure.
Moderator:	– roads you'd go to work on?
Vitter:	Three vital projects – I-49 North and South, I-10, the bridge in Baton Rouge – that is the mother of all traffic jams, it is the center of enormous problems in terms of quality of life here in the capital city – and other key infrastructure in high-growth areas like the River Parishes and Lake Charles. There are several important projects there…

United States, Uncivil

Edwards:	This program started off at 60 million dollars a year. It was recently at 250 million, went to 280 million this year, and it's going to be 400 million dollars a year in just a couple of years if we don't stop. And I am committed to stopping these tuition increases because they're pricing our kids out of higher education, they're making sure that our kids don't have the opportunity that they deserve to live the American dream right here in Louisiana. Now, we're going to increase our State General Fund support for higher ed. That's what we're going to do, Jackie, we're not going to have these tuition increases. And when we do that, overnight, TOPS becomes a sustainable program. We're not going to have to cap it. We're not going to have to invoke that statute that you just talked about. We're going to make sure that we do not increase the tuition on our students. TOPS is sustainable overnight.
Moderator:	Thank you very much.
Vitter:	Jackie, again, John Bel –
Moderator:	Thirty seconds.
Vitter:	John Bel says one thing in the campaign –
Edwards:	You know, Senator –
Vitter:	– and another in the legislature
Edwards:	– I didn't even mention your name there.

Vitter:	He supported five out of eight Jindal budgets. Those cut 330 million dollars from higher ed. He was part of that – not part of the solution, part of those cuts, part of that problem.
Edwards:	You supported Bobby Jindal three out of three elections –
Moderator:	Fifteen seconds.
Edwards:	– with your endorsements and your votes. Don't talk to me about supporting Bobby Jindal!
Moderator:	Quiet, gentlemen. Let's not –
Vitter:	John Bel…

The Generational Gap in Presidential Approval for Donald Trump

Patrick Fisher I *Seton Hall University*

This study examines the extremely large generation gap in support for Donald Trump. Unquestionably, the generational gap in Twenty-First century American politics predates Trump. Yet, prior to the 2016 presidential election, it was widely held that any potential Republican nominee for president would have to do considerably better among Millennials than John McCain and Mitt Romney to have a chance of winning the general election. Instead of trying to woo younger Americans, however, Donald Trump's campaign to "Make America Great Again" suggests that his campaign stoked fears about generational societal change, and in doing so, overtly focused on winning the votes of older Americans nostalgic for the country of their youth. Problematically, since generation correlates with other demographic characteristics, the generation gap is in Trump's support may simply be a result of other divisions in American politics, such as race, education, religion, and gender. A multivariate analysis utilizing data from the Pew Research Center, however, demonstrates this is not the case. Generation is a robust predictor of presidential approval for Trump on its own. Consequently, Trump's lack of appeal to younger Americans, after Barack Obama so successfully wooed them, has become a defining characteristic of contemporary American politics.

Patrick Fisher is a Professor of Political Science at Seton Hall University,
Patrick.Fisher@shu.edu

The Generational Gap in Presidential Approval for Donald Trump

The presidential election of 2016 was unlike any presidential election before it. Donald Trump, who few saw as a serious candidate when he announced he was running for president, astounded the political establishment by not only winning the Republican nomination but also winning the Electoral College in the general election. He did so despite the fact the fact that he had never held political office before and had the lowest recorded favorability rating of any major party presidential nominee in history, with exit polls indicating only 38% of the 2016 electorate had a favorable impression of him.

Trump won the presidency by presenting himself stylistically as a completely different candidate from previous presidential candidates. Trump's bluntness and lack of "political correctness" clearly appealed to many more voters than was imagined by the media and the political establishment when Trump first announced his run for the presidency. Trump victory was the result of him being able to make inroads in winning greater support of some demographic groups than previous Republican presidential nominees. The unique nature of Trump's unconventional campaign begs the question as to whether his appeal was the result of a generational transformation in the American electorate.

Unquestionably, the generational gap in Twenty-First century American politics predates Trump (see Figure 1). In the 2000 presidential election, the first generation before the Millennials began entering the electorate, there was a minimal generation gap. Since the Millennials began reaching voting age, however, this generation has been considerably more supportive of Democratic presidential nominees than older generations. The Millennial Generation's lack of support for Donald Trump in the 2016 election is thus consistent with their political behavior since the generation entered the electorate in notable numbers in 2004. In that election Millennials supported John Kerry by an 18-point margin, by far his best generation. Kerry's support among Millennials, however, was to a considerable degree a function of their contempt for George W. Bush rather than of strong support for Kerry himself (Jacobson, 2010). This, however, was not the case in 2008 and 2012 as Barack Obama himself was enormously popular among Millennials from the outset of him announcing his candidacy in 2007. The strong anti-Republican tendency of Millennials thus has its roots in the generation being both very pro-Obama and very anti-Bush. This was then reinforced by the fact that Trump himself proved to be extremely polarizing along generation lines during the 2016 campaign (Fisher, 2018).

Figure 1
Presidential Vote by Generation 2000-2016

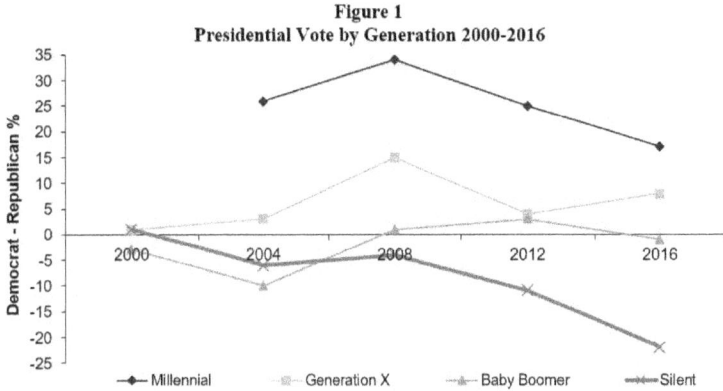

Generations are defined by the following birth years: *Generation Z*: adults born after 1996; *Millennial*: 1981 through 1996; *Generation X*: 1965 through 1980; *Baby Boomer*: 1946 through 1964; *Silent*: 1928 through 1945.
Source: American National Election Studies

Barack Obama's victories in the 2008 and 2012 elections were in a large part due to his overwhelming success among newly enfranchised Millennials. Republicans lack of support among Millennials was considered a key factor in the Party's losses to Obama. Without the Millennial vote, in fact, Obama would have lost reelection in 2012 (Fisher, 2014). After Obama's victories, it was widely held that any potential Republican nominee for president would have to do considerably better among younger voters than John McCain and Mitt Romney to have a chance of winning the general election. Instead of trying to woo younger Americans, however, Donald Trump's campaign to "Make America Great Again" suggests that his campaign stoked fears about generational societal change, and in doing so, overtly focused on winning the votes of older Americans nostalgic for the country of their youth. Consequently, Donald Trump did only marginally better among the younger American voters than the previous two Republican presidential nominees. As president, Trump's unpopularity among younger adults has, if anything, become even more pronounced. Trump's lack of appeal to younger Americans, after Obama so successfully wooed them, may now be a defining characteristic of contemporary American politics. This study will attempt to ascertain the reasons behind Trump's generation gap and the political implications of this generational divide.

Generations in American Politics

As long ago as 1970, it was shown that a statistical model was capable of explaining some of the underlying phenomena of generational effects (Carlsson and Karlsson, 1970). The political environment experienced by successive generations as they have come of age politically influences political attitudes throughout one's life. Consequently, societal changes that occur within a generation's life cycle have a bigger impact on the political views of younger people, who are still in the process of forming opinions. Older people are more likely to reflect the values prevalent when they are growing up. The greater acceptance of gay rights and interracial dating among young people than older ones today are examples of this (Frey, 2018).

When a life-cycle effect is at play, differences between younger and older people are largely due to their respective positions in the life cycle. For example, young people are far less likely than older Americans to vote and engage in politics. As people age, they vote at higher rates and their level of political engagement rises (Pew Research Center, 2015). The life-cycle explanation for the generation gap assumes that young persons are less affected by their social class than older person are because the young have had less experience in the work force than their elders and have had less time to learn the social and political norms of their class. The life-cycle explanation, however, has long found little empirical support (Abramson, 1975).

Differences between generations can also be conceptualized as the byproduct of the unique historical circumstances that members of an age cohort experience, particularly during a time when they are in the process of forming opinions. In some cases, this may be the result of a period effect an older generation experienced that subsequent generations did not (e.g. the younger generations of today did not experience the Vietnam War or the Civil Rights Movement because they were not yet born). In other cases, a historical moment can have an outsize effect on members of one generation. This may be because it occurs during a key point in the life cycle, such as adolescence and young adulthood, when awareness of the wider world deepens and personal identities and value systems are being strongly shaped (Pew Research Center, 2015). For example, persons born in the United States in 1920 spent their late adolescence and early adulthood in the Great Depression, whereas persons born just 10 years later spent the same stages of life in a period of relative prosperity and economic growth (Glenn, 2005).

Generations are a way to group age cohorts. A generation typically refers to groups of people born over a 15-20 year span. An age cohort spanning 15-20 years will necessarily include a diverse assortment of people, and often there are meaningful smaller cohorts within these generations. Changes in political circumstances, societal norms and economic conditions over a period of 15-20 years can lead to people within a cohort having different formative experiences (Pew Research Center, 2015).

The generational names we have chosen are the handiwork of popular culture, with some being drawn from a historic event, others from social or demographic change, and others from a turn in the calendar. Generational analysis in not an exact science and the years and terms that are used to define generations will vary from study to study. This study thus utilizes those generational boundaries and conceptions that are widely—though not universally—accepted (Pew Research Center, 2010). According to our definitions, each generation is similar in its longevity, ranging from 16 to 19 years in length. From oldest to youngest, the following parameters define the generations:

1) *The Silent Generation*, those born from 1928 through 1945; 2) *The Baby Boomers*, those born from 1946 through 1964; 3) *Generation X*, those born from 1965 through 1980; 4) *The Millennial Generation*, those born from 1981 through 1996, and 5) *Generation Z*, adults born after 1996.

A major influence on the political character of successive generations is the political climate and events that people in each generation experienced as they reached adulthood and began to form their political identities. The clearest pattern is that younger voters who became adults during the presidencies of Clinton, G.W. Bush, and Obama—the younger members of Gen X and the Millennial Generation—have typically voted much more Democratic than average. On the other hand, voters who became adults during the Ford, Carter, Reagan and G.H.W. Bush presidencies—much of Generation X and younger Baby Boomers—have tended to be somewhat more Republican than average. Those who turned 18 during the Nixon administration—a segment of older Baby Boomers—have tended to be slightly more Democratic than average in their voting. Those who came of age during the Eisenhower, Kennedy, and Johnson administrations—mostly members of the Silent Generation and the very oldest of the Baby Boomers—have tended to be distinctively more Republican than average. In contrast, before they died off, the generation that preceded the Silent Generation, the Greatest Generation, who came of age politically during the Franklin Roosevelt administration consistently voted more Democratic than average (Pew Research Center, 2011).

Thus, although there is a stereotype that younger Americans are always more liberal than older Americans are, this is not necessarily the case. In fact, in some years younger voters support more conservative candidates than older voters do. This was the case, for example, when Ronald Reagan won reelection by a landslide in 1984. Prior to the George W. Bush administration, most presidential elections since the advent of polling did not have much of an age gap, and by the 1990s there was evidence that the age gap on public policy issues that had grown in the 1960s and 1970s was shrinking (Fisher, 2014). At the end of the Twentieth Century, in fact, it was probably more accurate to view the country's oldest citizens as products of the New Deal, voters whose earliest memories lead them to have a lasting faith in the government activism and those more supportive of the Democratic Party. In the 1996 and 2000 presidential elections, for example, the oldest Americans were actually the age group most likely to vote Democratic.

The Generational Gap in Support for Donald Trump

The Pew Research Center in its "September 2018 Political Survey," which had a field period of September 18-24, 2018, asked respondents: "Do you approve or disapprove of the way Donald Trump is handling his job as President?" The responses to this question provide the basis for the analysis throughout the rest of this article. The generational gap on this question posed almost midway through Trump's four-year term in 2018 is consistent with the historical stereotype as younger Americans were considerably less likely to supportive of Trump than older Americans (see Figure 2). While 47% of Baby Boomers and the Silent Generation approved of Trump's performance in September 2018, less than one-third of Millennials and Generation Z approved. These figures do not represent a new trend. Though it is still too early to make historical inferences regarding Generation Z's political preferences, since Millennials have achieved adulthood and gained the right to vote, the generation has consistently been a generational outlier, giving considerably less support than other generations to Republican presidents and presidential candidates (Fisher, 2014).

Problematically, since generation correlates with other demographic characteristics, the generation gap in Trump's support may simply be a result of other divisions in American politics, such as race, gender, religion, education, and geography. We now turn to a discussion of these demographic factors as a counterpart to generation before presenting a multivariate analysis that demonstrates the significance of the generational gap in the era of Trump.

Figure 2
Presidential Approval for Donald Trump by Generation
September 2018
(%)

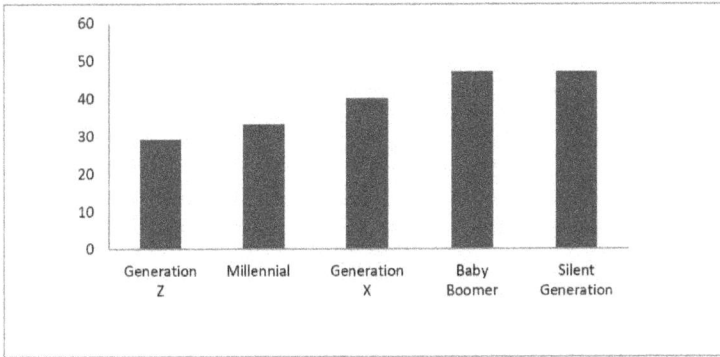

Generations are defined by the following birth years: *Generation Z*: adults born after 1996; *Millennial*: 1981 through 1996; *Generation X*: 1965 through 1980; *Baby Boomer*: 1946 through 1964; *Silent*: 1928 through 1945.
Source: Pew Research Center September 2018 Political Survey September 18-24, 2018.

The Generational Race Gap

Trump's campaign slogan "Make America Great Again" suggests that his campaign stoked fears about generational societal change. Many Trump supporters were deeply concerned that the country they live in is not the country of their youth and that they themselves were no longer represented by the U.S. government (Fisher, 2016). Support for Trump has thus been related to patriotism as Trump's supporters have asserted their "Americanness" as a distinct form of nationalism. Trump's appeal could thus be seen as more about a general intolerance of "others" and a rejection of out-groups than ideology and party identification. The Millennial Generation is considerably more diverse than older generations, especially the Silent Generation: among members of the Silent Generation, 79% are non-Hispanic whites; among the Millennial Generation, the figure is 59% and for Generation Z 52% (Pew Research Center, 2011; Fry and Parker, 2018).

The generational gap in support for Trump has thus in part been due to a reaction to older generations of the racial and ethnic diversity of Generation Z and the Millennial Generation and the change that signifies. But at the same time, it was a result of younger Americans being repelled by this message. Trump's poor performance among Gen Z and Millennials, therefore, should not be surprising as it can be regarded as a symptom of him actually running against what the younger generation of Americans represented.

An especially controversial aspect of Trump's populism that has not resonated with younger generations is the racial overtures of his appeals. Trump's appeals to racial resentment were consistent with his anti-intellectualism, a disparagement of the complexity associated with intellectual pursuits as a conservative form of populism that many Republicans have adopted since the 1960s (Shogan, 2007). Since Barry Goldwater won the Republican presidential nomination in 1964, Republicans have used race and increasingly immigration to attract white voters, especially working-class whites. This has led to an increasingly racially polarized polity as Republicans have had notable success appealing to older white Americans (Hajnal and Abrajano, 2016).

As Figure 3 displays, however, younger whites have been much less likely to be receptive to Trump's pitch. While nonwhites of all generations have given him tepid approval marks as president, among white voters there is a stark generation gap in Trump's approval. As president, white Millennials and Gen Zers have beem immune to Trump's charms: nearly midway through his presidential term less than two-fifths of whites in these generations approved of his performance as president. The difference among younger and older generations of whites is especially notable: a majority of whites in the Baby Boom and Silent Generation approved of his job as president in 2018, a clip of more than 10 points higher

Figure 3
Presidential Approval for Donald Trump by Generation and Race
September 2018
(%)

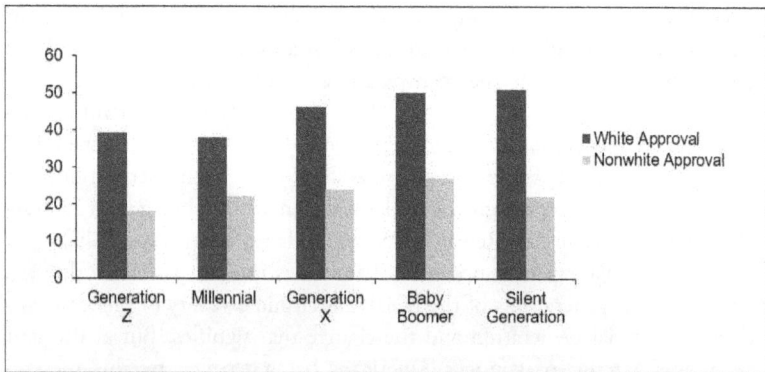

Generations are defined by the following birth years: *Generation Z*: adults born after 1996; *Millennial*: 1981 through 1996; *Generation X*: 1965 through 1980; *Baby Boomer*: 1946 through 1964; *Silent*: 1928 through 1945.
Source: Pew Research Center September 2018 Political Survey September 18-24, 2018.

than that of white Millennials and Gen Zers. Younger generations lack of support for Trump, therefore, was not just a symptom of the generations' relative racial and ethnic diversity.

Potentially part of the reason younger whites have been less supportive of Trump than older whites is due to their more tolerant attitudes toward immigration (Fisher, 2014). Trump's anti-immigration rhetoric mat be perceived to be a critical component of his success among older voters, but it repels many in the diverse younger generations. In the 2016 presidential election there was a strong relationship between the proportion of native born and support for Trump: relatively few people in the places where Trump was strong in 2016 were immigrants (Irwin and Katz, 2016). White Americans' concerns about Latinos and immigration have led to support for Trump's less generous and punitive policies that conflict with the preferences of much of the immigrant population. The country's growing racial diversity, therefore, is leading to a greater racial divide in politics. As whites move to the right of the political spectrum, racial minorities strongly support the left (Abrajano and Hajnal, 2015). Once elected president, Trump has, if anything, reinforced on his anti-immigrant message of his campaign and consequently his presidential approval ratings among Hispanics during the first year of his presidency was only 20% (Pew Research Center, 2017).

The Generational Gender Gap

Due to the historic candidacy of Hillary Clinton becoming the first female major party nominee for president, the gender gap received a considerable amount of attention during the 2016 campaign. Yet the gender gap, though large, was not considerably different from presidential elections since 2000 and was not nearly as pronounced as the generation gap. Clinton's inability to win white women voters, furthermore, crystalized how much more important race was than gender as a predictor of vote choice in 2016. On generational grounds, however, there has definitely gender differences of note regarding attitudes regarding the Trump presidency. All generations have gender gaps on Trump's approval of considerable size, with women in all generations at a dozen points less likely than men to approve of Trump (see Figure 4). Among younger women, however, Trump's approval ratings are especially weak: his approval ratings among women in Generation Z, the Millennial Generation, and Generation X all were less than 30%, and among Generation Z and Millennials it was closer to 20%. It is safe to say that younger women were not the target group of the "Make America Great Again" campaign message. Trump has consequently done particularly poorly among younger women. Of the five generations, the largest gender gap was among Generation X, where nearly twice as many male Gen Xers approved of Trump than females. Another way of looking at it is that Generation X men approved of Trump's performance as president at about the same level as Baby Boom and Silent Generation men while Trump's approval ratings among Generation X women were similar to those of Generation Z and the Millennial Generation. The country in the Trump era has unquestionably witnessed a huge generation-gender gap, one that received considerably less attention than the gender gap or generation gap on their own.

Figure 4
Presidential Approval for Donald Trump by Generation and Gender
September 2018
(%)

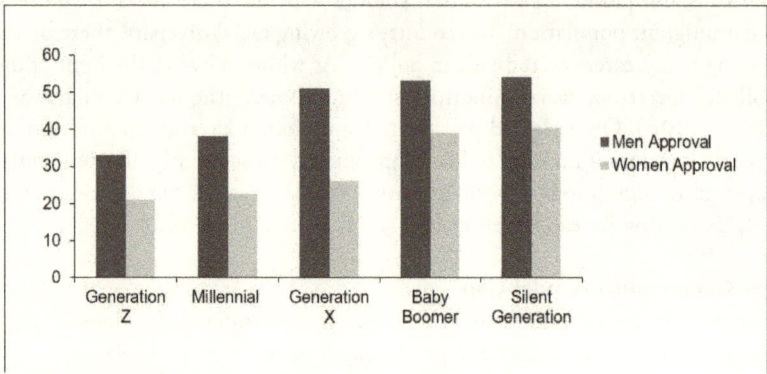

Generations are defined by the following birth years: *Generation Z*: adults born after 1996; *Millennial*: 1981 through 1996; *Generation X*: 1965 through 1980; *Baby Boomer*: 1946 through 1964; *Silent*: 1928 through 1945.
Source: Pew Research Center September 2018 Political Survey September 18-24, 2018.

Generation is thus an influential factor in the gender gap and the shifting political stances of women in the United States. Younger generations have become progressively more liberal and older generations more conservative; while this is not limited to gender, it is more apparent in women than men (Inglehart and Norris, 2000). Younger Americans have been born into generations where feminism is significantly more prominent and women's issues are accumulating extensive amounts of attention, and consequently they have aligned themselves with the less traditional, more progressive Democratic Party.

Younger women are more inclined to vote for the Democratic Party in part because they see the Party as sharing corresponding values and priorities on female-related issues. Differences in social welfare opinions may be the predominant contributor to the generational gender gap (Kaufmann and Petrocik, 1999). Yet many Republican and Evangelical women, two groups who voted overwhelmingly for Trump, accept and even endorse the kind of gender inequalities that are embodied by Trump (Strolovitch, Wong and Proctor, 2017). Younger women, however, are considerably less likely to identify themselves as either Republican or Evangelical than older females.

The large generation-gender gap that has emerged on presidential approval for Trump has impacted attitudes towards the parties. A year into the Trump presidency, only 23% of female Millennials and Gen Zers identified as Republicans or leaned Republican while 70% claimed to be a Democrat or to lean Democratic (Pew Research Center, 2018). With Trump's election, Millennial women who were strongly Democratic beforehand have been becoming even more so: in the second term of the Obama administration 56% of Millennial women identified or leaned Democratic. About half of Millennial men, on the other hand, align with the Democratic Party, little changed in recent years.

The Generational Religion Gap
Trump's "Make America Great Again" message also suggests a nostalgia for an era where religion was more important in people's lives and more Americans were conservative on social issues that divide the country today. Consequently, Trump's poor approval ratings among younger Americans may also be a product of Generation Z's and Millennials' relative lack of religiosity and the social liberalism that corresponds with it. Younger generations are considerably less likely to attend religious service than those of other generations, especially the Silent Generation (Fisher, 2014). While almost one-half of younger Americans never attend religious services, the figure is less than one-third for the Silent Generation. Almost one-half of the Silent Generation, on the other hand, attends religious services at least weekly, a figure that is more than twice that of younger Americans. As Figure 5 displays, there is a considerable generation gap in support for Trump based on attendance of religious services. Of the five generations, only the Silent Generation did not have a notable generation-religious gap. Among younger Americans who do not regularly attend religious services, Trump was especially unpopular. Of non-religious Millennials and Gen Xers less than one-third approved of Trump and for Gen Zers figure was only about one-sixth.

Figure 5
Presidential Approval for Donald Trump by Generation and Religious Attendance
September 2018
(%)

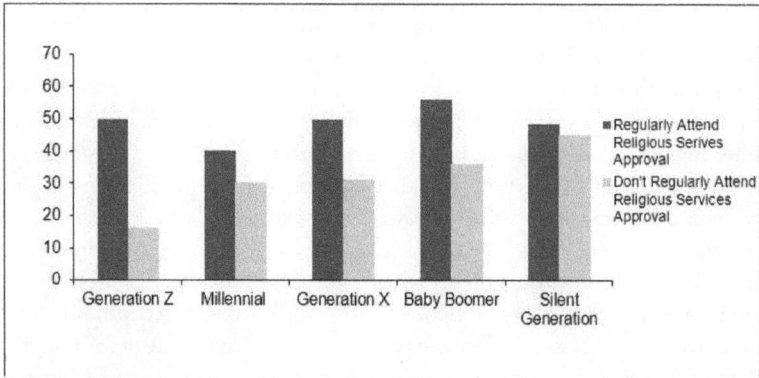

Generations are defined by the following birth years: *Generation Z*: adults born after 1996; *Millennial*: 1981 through 1996; *Generation X*: 1965 through 1980; *Baby Boomer*: 1946 through 1964; *Silent*: 1928 through 1945.
Attends Religious Services includes those who attend more than once a week, once a week, once or twice a year, and a few times a year; Don't Attend Religious Services includes those who attend seldom or never.
Source: Pew Research Center September 2018 Political Survey September 18-24, 2018.

Younger Americans relative lack of religiosity has particularly had an important impact on the generation's views on social issues that have a much more important impact on vote choice than used to be the case. Younger generations are consistently to the left of older Americans on social issues, on some (e.g. gay marriage) by huge margins and are more likely to say that Democrats, rather than Republicans, come closer to sharing their moral values (Fisher, 2014). Younger Americans with comparatively liberal social views are unlikely to see themselves in a party in which large and vocal segments favor constitutional bans on abortion and same-sex marriage, reject evolution, and deny the reality of human-induced global warming (Jacobson, 2009).

Since the 1990s there has been a greater emphasis placed on cultural issues by candidates and other political elites (Mann and Ornstein, 2012). Moral traditionalism has thus exerted a greater effect on vote choice through party identification and there has been a process of realignment in the electorate along a moral traditionalism divide. Consequently, younger Americans have turned away from organized religion because they perceive it as deeply entangled with conservative politics (Taylor, 2015). The religiously unaffiliated have become among the most reliably Democratic segments of the electorate. Moreover, they constitute a growing share of the Democratic electoral base. This insinuates a widening and deepening of a cultural-values-based realignment of the American electorate.

The Generational Education Gap

Younger generations have notably higher education levels than older Americans. A third of Millennials over the age of 25 have a four-year degree or more—making them the best educated cohort of young adults in American history. Though the generation's young age has limited the number that have finished graduate school, more Millennials have already have gone to college and gradated high school than the Silent Generation (Fisher, 2018). As Figure 6 demonstrates, the education gap goes hand-and-hand with the generation gap regarding Trump's presidential approval. Though in 2018 Generation Z was still too young to produce a cohort of college graduates making it too early to compare political differences among different education levels of the generation, among Millennials there was a marked gap on Trump approval along educational levels as only about one-in-four college-educated Millennials approved of his presidential performance. Conversely, about one-half of those in the Baby Boom and Silent Generation without a college degree approved of his performance in September 2018. For every generation, those with a college degree were

Figure 6
Presidential Approval for Trump by Generation and Education
September 2018
(%)

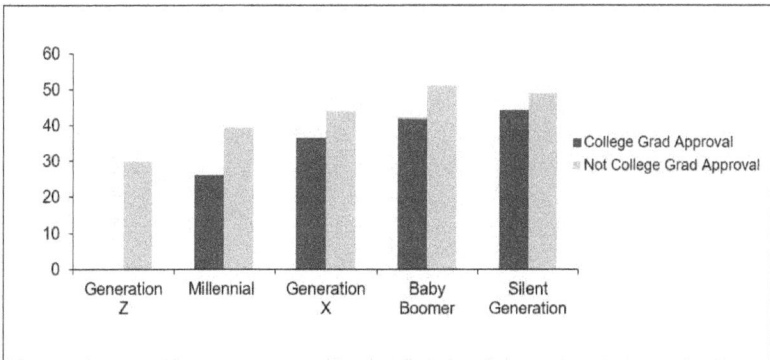

Generations are defined by the following birth years: *Generation Z*: adults born after 1996; *Millennial*: 1981 through 1996; *Generation X*: 1965 through 1980; *Baby Boomer*: 1946 through 1964; *Silent*: 1928 through 1945.
Source: Pew Research Center September 2018 Political Survey September 18-24, 2018.

considerably less supportive of Trump than those without a college degree. The emerging importance of education in Americans' electoral choices may be due to the development of partisanship as a form of social identification and parties as extensive social networks. As younger American adults age and an even great number do post-baccalaureate studies, the generational divide on educational grounds may even intensify.

Trump has fared especially poorly among those attaining post-grad degrees: in his first year as president only 22% of those with post-grad education levels approved of his performance (Pew Research Center, 2017). Educational attainment is now potentially a better indicator of long-term economic well-being than household incomes. Unionized jobs in the auto industry, for example, pay reasonably well even if they do not require college degrees. These jobs, however, are also potentially at risk of automation of moving overseas. From a generational perspective this is important because younger Americans are less likely to be working in jobs that are at risked of leaving the country.

Trump's populism is thus in many regards a poor match for the Millennials and Gen Zers. As the first generations raised on the internet, Millennials and Gen Zers have developed a distinctly global perspective. These well-educated generations have been exposed to much more of the world, both in terms of technology and in terms of personal travel and are much more likely to have a global outlook that Trump disdains. In the 2016 presidential election, Trump tended to do best in counties where white identity mixes with low education levels. His supporters were disproportionately from areas of the county that largely missed the transition of the United States away from manufacturing and into a diverse, information-driven globalized economy. Trump did better in areas of the country with high concentrations of whites without a high school diploma, in areas where many self-describe themselves as ancestrally "American," and areas with high percentages living in a mobile home (Irwin and Katz, 2016). These areas also tend to be considerably older than the country as a whole, with relatively few Millennials and Gen Zers.

The Generational Urbanism Gap

Place identity is important in U.S. politics (Cramer, 2016). Where one lives has an important influence on one's political attitudes. The existence of an urbanism gap in American culture and politics is one of the oldest concepts in the study of American politics and there has long been a strong relationship between population density and political beliefs (Key, 1955). There are important differences in identity politics and political culture along geographical lines, and as president Trump has tried to exploit these differences. From a partisan perspective, Republicans today tend to live in areas where people are farther apart, and Democrats tend to cluster in places where people live closer together (Bishop, 2008). As a result of population movement, immigration, and party realignment within the electorate, Republicans are increasingly surrounded by other Republicans and Democrats by other Democrats (Abramowitz, 2018).

Though the urbanism gap in support for Donald Trump exists for all generations, there are some generational dynamics of note (see Figure 7). For the generational bookends of Generation Z and the Silent Generation, the urbanism gap in support for Trump is relatively small, within single digits. For the Millennials and Baby Boomers, the gap is larger, in the teens. For Generation X, however, the urbanism gap is noticeably larger than for the other generations, with Generation Xers in nonurban areas supporting Trump by more than twice the level of those in urban areas.

Figure 7
Presidential Approval for Trump by Generation and Urbanism
September 2018
(%)

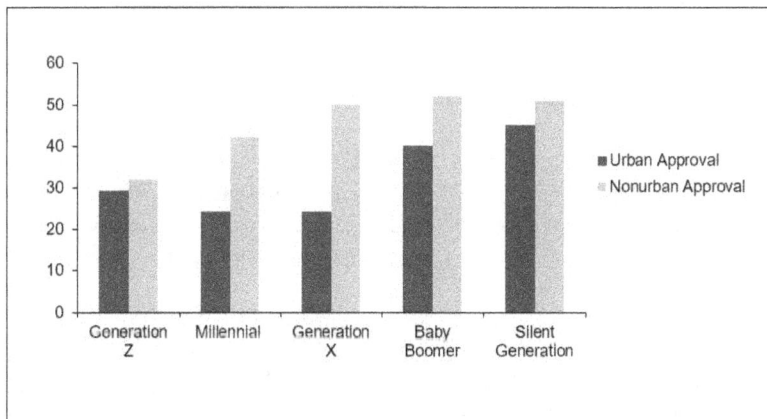

Generations are defined by the following birth years: *Generation Z*: adults born after 1996; *Millennial*: 1981 through 1996; *Generation X*: 1965 through 1980; *Baby Boomer*: 1946 through 1964; *Silent*: 1928 through 1945.
Source: Pew Research Center September 2018 Political Survey September 18-24, 2018.

A logical reason for the urbanism gap is that there are obvious demographic differences between urban and nonurban areas of the country. Nonurban (rural and suburban) areas tend to be whiter and poorer and to have lower education levels, more married couples, and more churchgoers than highly populated urban areas. Not only do nonurban populations tend to be more heterogeneous racially, ethnically, religiously, and culturally than urban areas, but urban areas are also, on the whole, younger. The urbanism gap thus may be in part a consequence of generational differences. The country has not been aging uniformly by place of residence. This is at least partially due to factors such as increased life expectancy, migration of younger workers to cities, and the flow of older people toward more rural areas. The gap between the younger urban areas of the country and the older nonurban areas has widened slightly in the past thirty years and seems poised to continue to do so (Kirschner, Berry, and Glasgow, 2006). The urbanism gap is consequently a defining feature of the cultural wars in contemporary American politics. Nonurban voters own more guns, are more likely to oppose abortion rights, and have more traditional family arrangements than those living elsewhere (Fisher, 2014). This suggests that nonurban voters share some set of inherent values with each other that leads them to be more supportive of Donald Trump.

Multivariate Analysis

Since there is such a strong relationship between generation and other demographic characteristics, it is possible that the generation gap in Trump's support is simply be a result of other demographic divisions in American politics. To test for this possibility, a multivariate analysis was conducted to demonstrate the degree by which generation stands alone has as a demographic predictor in contemporary U.S. politics. As was the case in the previously examined generational demographic gaps, the multivariate analysis for presidential approval for Trump employed the database made available by the Pew Research Center in its "September 2018 Political Survey," which had a field period of September 18-24, 2018.

Table 1 contains the results of a binary logic regression model predicting the likelihood of presidential approval of Donald Trump, with the model including generation cohorts as independent variables as well as the aforementioned demographic variables of race, gender, religion, education, and urbanism. Since contemporary American politics is so partisan and Trump has consistently maintained impressive levels of support among Republicans (Gramlich, 2019), partisan identification is also included as an independent variable to determine the degree by which generational approval for Trump is different from base partisanship. To test generational effect, the model includes the generational cohorts of Generation Z/Millennial and Generation X, while the Baby Boomer/ Silent Generation cohort is used as the baseline and left out of the model.

Table 1. Significance of Demographic Gaps on Presidential Approval in 2018

	Coefficient	Wald
Race	0.969***	35.186
	(0.163)	
Gender	0.764***	30.090
	(0.139)	
Religion	0.835***	36.658
	(0.138)	
Education	−0.598***	19.451
	(0.136)	
Urbanism	−0.543***	14.203
	(0.144)	
Party	−3.378***	245.039
	(0.216)	
Gen Z/Millennial	−0.599***	12.251
	(0.171)	
Generation X	−0.359*	4.583
	(0.168)	
Constant	−0.386	3.262
	(0.214)	
Nagelkerke R^2	.494	
Cases Predicted Correctly	82.1%	

Notes:

[1] Binary logistic regression estimates (1 = Approval for Donald Trump) with standard errors in parentheses;

[2] Standard errors in parentheses;

[3] Significance levels: ∗ : 5% hspace.5em∗ ∗ ∗ : .1%;

[4] Dependent Variable: Approval of Donald Trump in 2018 (1 = Approve of Trump Handling of Presidency, 0 = Disapproval of Trump Handling of Presidency/Don't Know/Refused);

[5] Independent Variables: 1) Race = Respondent's Race (1= White, 0 = Non-White); 2) Gender = Respondent's Gender (1 = Male, 0 = Female); 3) Religion = Religious Services Attendance (1 = Attend Religious Services Regularly/Occasionally, 0 = Never Attend Religious Services); 4) Education = Respondent's Education Level (1 = College Degree, 0 = No College Degree); 5) Urbanism = Respondent's Place of Residence (1= Urban, 0 = Non-urban); 6) Party = Respondent's Party Identification (1 = Democrat, 0 = Other); 7) Generation Z/Millennial = Respondent's Generation (1=Generation Z or Millennial, 0 = Other); 8) Generation X = Respondent's Generation (1= Generation X, 0 = Other);

[6] Source: Pew Research Center September 2018 Political Survey September 18-24, 2018.

Generation, the model indicates, is a strong predictor of presidential approval of Donald Trump. Controlling for other demographic factors and partisanship, one's generation was statistically significant independent variable. Using the Baby Boom/Silent Generation cohort as the baseline, the Generation Z/Millennial generational cohort was statistically significant at p < .001 and Generation X was statistically significant at p < .05.

In terms of size effects of the independent variables, party identification unsurprisingly shows by far the largest size effect. After partisanship, however, the size effect of the Generation Z/Millennial generational cohort in particular (Generation X less so) is comparable to some of the other independent variables, all of which are significant at p < .001. After party, the largest size effects are church attendance, race, and gender. Regular church attenders are much more likely to approve of Trump than nonregular attenders, whites are considerably more supportive of President Trump than nonwhites, and men are more likely to approve of his presidential performance than women. The Generation Z/ Millennial independent variable had a size effect rivalling that of the college and urbanism independent variables. College graduates are significantly less supportive of Trump than those with lower levels of educational attainment and Trump's approval rating is considerably worse among those living in urban areas as opposed to nonurban areas. Overall the model predicted over 80 percent of the cases correctly, indicating just how strong demographic factors—including generation—are in predicting whether one approves of Trump's performance as president.

From a generational perspective, the key finding of the multivariate analysis is that younger Americans are notably less supportive of Donald Trump than older generational cohorts. The younger one's generation, the less likely one is to approve of Trump's presidency. The strong negative coefficients of the generational cohorts tested in the model also indicates that those in the Baby Boom and Silent generations are considerably more likely to approve of Trump's presidential performance. Overall, therefore, the model indicates that the adult generational "bookends" today—Generation Z/Millennial and Baby Boomer/ Silent—were especially strong predictors of support for Trump. Whether or not one is a member of the contemporary middle generation of Generation X, on the other hand, did not have as marked of an influence on the model (though, again, it was still statistically significant at p < .05). The model thus underlines that whether one was a member of the youngest two or oldest two generations of American adults was an important determinant of presidential approval of Trump. Consequently, the multivariate analysis demonstrates that generation was a robust predictor of Trump approval on its own.

The fact that it was the youngest and oldest generational cohorts that were stronger generational predictors, rather than Generation X, has important implications regarding the future of American politics. It suggests the possibility of heightened potential consequences of generational replacement as the generations that are the strongest supporters of Donald Trump today, the Baby Boom and Silent generations, are replaced in the electorate by a generation that are the anti-Trump outliers, Generation Z and the Millennial Generation. If history is any guide, as younger voters mature they will vote at increasingly higher rates and they will generally maintain their original partisan loyalties (Fisher, 2014). The antipathy of the Millennials and Gen Zers toward Donald Trump, therefore, potentially will have a long-term impact on American politics.

Conclusion

This study insinuates a couple noteworthy conclusions. First, one's generation was an important determinant of whether one approved of the way that Trump was handling his job as president in September 2018. To be sure, there was a strong correlation between generation and presidential approval. Younger generations are much less supportive of Donald Trump than older generations. Second, the link between generation and presidential approval for Donald Trump remains strong even when controlling for a host of other demographic factors. Indeed, the effect of generation on support for Donald Trump is robust enough that it does not "wash out" in the presence of additional covariates.

What are the consequences of Trump's generational gap? The last half century has seen dramatic demographic, social, and technological changes and different generations of Americans have their own distinct reactions to these changes. The racial and ethnic makeup of the country has been transformed. Trump's victory in 2016 was in part due to generational divide on the transformations the country has witnessed. In general, older generations are having a harder time processing these changes, while younger generations are more likely to take them in stride. Among older Americans, there is a tension between their belief that America is the greatest country in the world and a sense of pessimism about the country's future. Younger Americans are less convinced about America's greatness but more comfortable with the path the country is currently on (Pew Research Center, 2011).

Americans partisan identities motivate them far more powerfully than their view about issues. Although Americans may insist in the importance of values and ideologies in their vote choice, they actually care less about policy and more that their party wins (Mason, 2014). Though it is possible that Trump could help ideologically redefine the Republican Party in a way that appeals to more voters in the future, Trump's lack of appeal among younger Americans poses considerable risk for Republicans long-term. There is the distinct possibility that Trump's agenda may be too backward looking to win new supporters in future elections. His call to "Make America Great Again" appeals openly to nostalgia. He won in 2016 by maximizing the support in decisive states among declining segments of the electorate: older, rural, white, non-college-educated voters

(Harwood, 2017). In other words, Trump's base of support was everything that the Millennial Generation and Generation Z are not. And as demonstrated by this study's analysis of Trump's approval ratings, the generational divide of the 2016 election has continued to be pronounced after his inauguration.

Donald Trump's style and tactics—as well as his political message—has encouraged a widening of the generational gap in American politics. The unpopularity of Trump among younger American adults, combined with the tremendous support Barack Obama managed to garner among younger voters during his presidency, has created a new overwhelmingly Democratic generation of voters. As the political power of Millennials and Generation Z grows in stature through generational replacement, long-term demographic trends suggest that Donald Trump's strategy of highlighting generational resentment, though successful in 2016, may come back to eventually haunt the Republican Party.

References

Abrajano, Marisa and Zoltan L. Hajnal. 2015. *White Backlash: Immigration, Race, and American Politics.* Princeton, NJ: Princeton University Press.

Abramowitz, Alan. 2018. *The Great Alignment.* New Haven: Yale.

Abramson, Paul R. 1975. *Generational Change in American Politics.* Lexington, MA: Lexington Books.

Almond, Gabriel and Sidney Verba. 1965. *The Civic Culture.* Boston: Little, Brown.

Bishop, Bill. 2008. *The Big Sort.* Boston: Houghton Mifflin.

Carlsson, Gosta, and Katarina Karlsson. 1970. "Age, Cohorts and the Generation of Generations." *American Sociological Review* 35: 710-718.

Cramer, Katherine. 2016. *The Politics of Resentment.* Chicago: University of Chicago Press.

Fisher, Patrick. 2014. *Demographic Gaps in American Political Behavior.* Boulder, CO: Westview Press.

Fisher, Patrick. 2016. "Definitely Not Moralistic: State Political Culture and Support for Donald Trump in the Race for the 2016 Republican Presidential Nomination." *PS: Political Science and Politics* 49: 743-747.

Fisher, Patrick. 2018. "A Political Outlier: The Distinct Politics of the Millennial Generation." *Society* 55: 35-40.

Frey, William. 2018. "Race, Aging, and Politics: America's Cultural Generation Gap." *Public Policy and Aging Report* 28: 9-13.

Fry, Richard. 2016. "Millennials Match Baby Boomers as Largest Generation in U.S. Electorate, but Will They Vote?" *Pew Research Center*, May 16.

Fry, Richard and Kim Parker. 2018. "Early Benchmarks Show 'Post-Millennials' on Track to Be Most Diverse, Best-Educated Generation Yet." *Pew Research Center*, November 15.

Glenn, Norval D. 2005. *Cohort Analysis.* Thousand Oaks, CA: Sage Publications.

Gramlich, John. 2019. "Partisans Agree Political Leaders Should be Honest and Ethical, Disagree Whether Trump Fits the Bill." *Pew Research Center*, January 30.

Hajnal, Zoltan and Marisa Abrajano. 2016. "Trump's All Too Familiar Strategy and Its Future in the GOP." *The Forum* 14: 295-309.

Harwood, John. 2017. "Why Trumpism May Not Endure." *New York Times* January 21.

Inglehart, Ronald, and Norris, Pippa. 2000. "The Developmental Theory of the Gender Gap: Women's and Men's Voting Behavior in Global Perspective." *International Political Science Review* 21: 441-463.

Irwin, Neil and Josh Katz. 2016. "The Geography of Trumpism." *New York Times* March 12.

Jacobson, Gary. 2009. "The Effects of the George W. Bush Presidency on Partisan Attitudes." *Presidential Studies Quarterly* 39: 172–209.

Jacobson, Gary. 2010. *A Divider, Not a Uniter.* New York: Pearson.

Kauffmann, Karen M. and John R. Petrocik. 1999. "The Changing Politics of American Men: Understanding the Sources of the Gender Gap." *American Journal of Political Science* 43: 864-887.

Key, V.O. 1955. "A Theory of Critical Elections." *Journal of Politics* 17: 3-18.

Kirschner, Annabelle E. Helen Berry, and Nina Glasgow. 2006. "The Changing Faces of Rural America," in *Population Change and Rural Society*, eds. William Kandel and David Brown, pp. 53-74. New York: Springer Books.

Koch, Jeffrey W. 2003. "Political Cynicism and Third-Party Support in American Presidential Elections." *American Politics Research* 31: 48-65.

Mann, Thomas E., and Norman J. Ornstein. 2012. *It's Even Worse Than It Looks: How the American Constitutional System Collided with the New Politics of Extremism.* New York: Basic Books.

Mason, Lilliana. 2014. "Why People Vote Republican but Support Liberal Policies." *The Washington Post* November 21.

Pew Research Center. 2010. "The Millennials: Confident. Connected. Open to Change." February 24.

Pew Research Center. 2011. "The Generation Gap and the 2012 Election." November 3.

Pew Research Center. 2015. "The Whys and Hows of Generations Research." September 3.

Pew Research Center. 2017. "Presidential Approval June 2017." June 20.

Pew Research Center. 2018. "Wide Gender Gap, Growing Educational Divide in Voters' Party Identification." March 20.

Shogan, Colleen J. 2007. "Anti-Intellectualism in the Modern Presidency." *Perspectives on Politics* 5: 295-303.

Strolovitch, Dara Z., Janelle S. Wong, and Andrew Proctor. 2017. "A Possessive Investment in White Heteropatriarchy? The 2016 Election and the Politics of Race, Gender, and Sexuality." *Politics, Groups, and Identities* 5: 353-363.

Taylor, Paul. 2015. *The Next America*. New York: Public Affairs.

The Impact of Racial Fear on Attitudes Toward Gun Control

Emily Ready | *College of William & Mary*

Racial fear and gun control are two politically salient issues that appear to be related in ways not fully understood. I examine this relationship by focusing on guns as a means of self-defense against different nationalities that may be perceived as threatening to some American citizens. Using a variety of statistical techniques, I find first that an explicit measure of racial fear exerts no significant effect on preferences for wider access to concealed-carry permits, likely attenuated by social desirability bias. Yet, support for increased border security and opposing admittance of Syrian refugees as proxies for racial fear significantly and substantially increase the likelihood of supporting increased access to concealed-carry permits, in line with expectations.

Emily Ready is a senior Government major at the College of William & Mary. Her research interests lie at the intersection of public opinion and quantitative methodology, egready@email.wm.edu. The author would like to thank Philip Waggoner for his immense guidance and support throughout this process. The author would also like to thank the Cooperative Congressional Election Survey for making their survey data available to the public. All mistakes remain the author's own.

Introduction

In 2016, there were 11,000 gun-related homicides and 384 mass shootings in the U.S. (Jeffrey, 2018; Rhodan, 2017). From 1966 to 2012, 31% of the world's mass shootings occurred on U.S. soil. Despite these trends, the U.S. continues to own the most guns per capita of any country in the world (Willingham and Saeed, 2017). At the same time, but on a different dimension, issues involving race are becoming increasingly prominent. For example, there exists significant opposition to illegal immigration as well as accepting refugees from the Middle East. A Pew Research Center 2019 poll found that 40% of Americans favor "substantially expanding the wall along the U.S. border with Mexico," and a 2017 poll found that 46% of Americans "said 'a large number of refugees leaving countries such as Iraq and Syria' was a major threat to the well-being of the U.S." (Gramlich, 2019; Smith, 2017). Further, racial tension has experienced a recent resurgence, seen, for example, in the shooting of unarmed minorities. An analysis by *The Guardian* found that in 2015, despite making up only 37.4% of the U.S. population, non-white Americans made up 62.7% of the victims in unarmed police shootings (Swaine, Laughland, and Lartey, 2015). In light of some shared themes in these two realms of opposition to gun control and an increase in racial fear, I am interested in exploring the relationship between these two concepts.

Extant work, which is reviewed in the following section, has explored the theoretical antecedents to racial fear and racial fear's relation to gun control. Building on these works, but in light of the rapidly changing political and social landscapes, scholarship would benefit from an updated theoretical and empirical study on the subject. Further, considering how controversial issues regarding other races and ethnicities have become, specifically in the realms of illegal immigration and political postures towards Syrian refugees discussed above, it is important to take these new issues into account when exploring drivers of gun-related attitudes.

Using the 2016 Cooperative Congressional Election Survey (CCES) and a variety of statistical techniques, I found that both supporting increased border security and opposing admittance of Syrian refugees increase the likelihood of supporting easier access to concealed-carry permits. The "racial fear" measure leveraged in this study was statistically insignificant in predicting support for concealed-carry permits. These findings provide some insight into understanding political behavior and mass policy preferences for a variety of reasons. Bias towards various nationalities exists, and by using support for increased border security and opposition towards admitting Syrian refugees as proxies for racial fear, this bias appears to be, at least in part, one of the driving forces in the pro-gun movement in the U.S. This is a relatively conservative look at this relationship, yet still valuable, as by using this knowledge policymakers could craft policies aimed specifically at reducing racial bias, possibly increasing support for policies that would reduce gun violence. In this paper, I first summarize the relevant literature on these subjects. Next, I detail my theory that opinions towards certain policy issues involving race are significantly related to attitudes towards gun control. My expectation is that individuals who are racially fearful are more resistant to gun-control, given the linkage between guns, a sense of safety, and the driver of fear. In addition to an explicit measure of racial fear, I explore two proxies for racial fear including support for increased U.S.-Mexican border security and also opposition towards allowing Syrian refugees into the U.S. Specifically, individuals who oppose admittance of Syrian refugees into the U.S. should be more likely to support increased access to concealed-carry permits. I expect the same outcome for individuals who support increased border security. Upon specifying my theory and hypotheses, I present my data and methods for testing these expectations. Upon presenting and discussing my results as well as robustness of these models, I conclude by discussing limitations of my approach and how my study can be expanded for future projects.

Literature Review
In examining how an individual's racial fear and attitudes toward certain issues involving race influence that individual's opinion of easier access to concealed-carry permits, a good starting point is focusing on the social identity of American citizens, as that is the group I am studying. Mangum and Block's (2018) theory provides evidence that suggests some Americans are prejudiced towards those unlike them. Analyzing data from the 2004-2005 National Politics Survey, they found that American citizens possess an "American identity," which enables them to "place those they believe do not have an American identity in the out-group" (Mangum and Block, 2018, 2). "Sociopolitical threat" and "sociocultural threat," were found to trend negatively with American identity, meaning that individuals thought to be a political or cultural threat were more likely to be seen as un-American (Mangum and Block, 2018, 7). These two factors are specifically related to distrust of outsiders, as citizens may view them as threatening the political and cultural status-quo. However, this distrust may be unnoticed by the in-group, resulting in implicit bias (Banks and Hicks, 2015; Culotta, 2012). Implicit prejudice towards others "can cause [the in-group] to evaluate and act more negatively to [the out-group]" than conscious prejudice (Banks and Hicks, 2015, 641). According to Pehrson, Brown, and

Zagefka's (2009) study, when these in-groups are conceptualized by participants as based on ethnicity, they are more likely to have negative feelings towards immigrants, specifically asylum-seekers.

Refugees and immigrants have consistently been cited as out-groups in the eyes of Americans. Muslims have been susceptible to racial violence and prejudice, especially after 9/11/2001 (Disha, Cavendish, and King, 2011; Kaplan, 2007; Rabrenovic, 2007). Many scholars have labeled this racism "Islamophobia" in response to how prevalent these attitudes are in society (Kaplan, 2007; Ogan, Willnat, Pennington, and Bashir, 2014; Rana, 2007; Romero and Zarrugh, 2018; Zaal, 2012). Fadda-Conrey (2011) argues that prejudice against Muslims was present before 9/11, as a result of international crises that centered around the Middle East. These events and 9/11 have formed a Muslim stereotype that labels them as violent and against American values. Bhatia (2015, iii) found that even if their personal interactions with Muslims were positive, American evangelicals still viewed Islam as "an evil religion." This stereotype has seemed to affect refugees coming into the U.S. Refugees from areas where Islam is the prevailing religion tend to experience more hate than empathy, to the point of being dehumanized (Bruneau, Kteily, and Laustsen, 2017). The Muslim stereotype and Islamophobia have also affected how Americans see other foreigners. By analyzing government and media reports and data, Romero and Zarrugh (2018) discovered that Islamophobia, and similar rhetoric against terrorism, has been used as justification to increase border security.

Immigrants to the U.S. have faced similar racism, specifically those illegally crossing the U.S.-Mexican border. These immigrants are associated with violence, as suggested by Bassett and Connelly's (2011) experiment. Subjects were prompted to be aware of their mortality by responding to a fear of death scale, and this prompting caused more negative reactions toward a passage about an illegal Mexican immigrant compared to a passage about an illegal Canadian immigrant. Additionally, how these immigrants are labeled affects society's perception of them. For example, the term "illegal alien" increases perceptions of threat in individuals, as opposed to the term "undocumented worker" (Pearson, 2010).

Regarding gun ownership, a general consensus among scholars is that ownership is largely driven by fear of others. A Pew Research Center 2017 poll found that 67% of gun owners cite protection as the main reason for owning a gun (Igielink and Brown, 2017). Additionally, individuals with a fear of crime are more likely to own or purchase a gun for self-defense (Cao, Cullen, and Link, 2006; Hauser and Kleck, 2013). McDowall and Loftin (1983, 1147) theorized that "legal handgun demand is responsive to evaluations of the strength of collective security," observing that demand for handguns increased when the number of riots and crime rates increased and when the number of "resources devoted to collective security," including the number of police per capita, decreased. This response to collective security, provided by the state, suggests that individuals place some trust in government when it provides protection. Informal collective security, or an individual's belief that the people around them will help prevent violence, also reduces gun ownership for self-defense purposes (Cao, Cullen, and Link, 2006).

Authors have attributed gun ownership and the accompanying desire for protection to a "fear of the other," finding that much of this fear has been racialized by past events, such as blacks gaining political power, 9/11, and the recent recession in 2008 (Cramer, 1994; Waugaman, 2016). Regardless of specific events, O'Brien, Forrest, Lynott, and Daly (2013) found that the odds of a white individual owning a gun increased with symbolic racism, not specific prejudice against one group. Filindra and Kaplan (2016) strengthen these theories by determining that "racial resentment is a statistically significant and substantively important predictor of white opposition to gun control" (255).

Gun advocacy groups, namely the National Rifle Association (NRA), have been found to capitalize on this fear of the other. Bhatia (2019) found that "the NRA's 'disinformation campaign reliant on fearmongering' is constructed around a narrative of 'fear and identity politics' that exploits current xenophobic sentiments related to immigrants" (Pierre, 2019). The NRA has also been found to use religious rhetoric in their promotions so as to align gun rights with the Christian Moral Majority that arose in the 1970s (Dawson, 2019).

Theoretical Context

In this paper, it is my goal to explain how racial fear, specifically opposition towards accepting refugees from Syria and support for increased border security at the U.S.-Mexican border, influence supporting easier access to concealed-carry permits. In pursuit of this goal, several assumptions are made about how the actors perceive these concepts. My first assumption is that support for easier access to concealed-carry permits reflects a desire to make guns more accessible to the public. One of the main arguments behind the pro-gun position is that it would be easier to neutralize those inciting violence if responsible citizens were armed. This logic suggests that those who want easier access to concealed-carry expect there to be situations where self-defense is necessary in public. They may perceive guns as a way to further protect themselves and others from potential harm. This perception is supported by social norms in the U.S. that promote guns being used for self-defense purposes, such as police officers carrying them. The question I am attempting to answer is whether this perception of guns is a possible response to racial fear and opinions towards specific issues involving race.

Racial fear is captured by respondents' levels of acceptance toward other races. By acknowledging that they have a level of racial fear, respondents are admitting that they are afraid of other races and are therefore unlikely to be accepting towards them. However, this variable is problematic because it is closely tied to social desirability bias (Berinsky, 2004). Because of the well-founded negative social impact being labeled a "racist" brings, some respondents could not be truthful in their response, or may feel uncomfortable answering the question. Respondents may also not realize that they have these prejudices. For these reasons, proxies for racial fear may reveal patterns unable to be observed when looking at an explicit measure of racial fear. As such, for these proxies for racial fear, I look at opposition to admitting Syrian refugees and support for increasing border security along the U.S-Mexican border.

Because admitting Syrian refugees and border security are issues related to policy, it should be easier for people to form and express an opinion on them than general racial fear. Policy questions are posed as doing what is best for the country. Rejecting a group of people may be easier to justify on these grounds, rather than because of who they are or where they are from. This should make opposition to admitting Syrian refugees and support for increasing border security more accurate measurements of respondents' true opinions than level of racial fear.

Opposition towards admitting Syrian refugees and support for increased border control may currently be attributable to other concerns besides racial fear, such as that immigrants will put a burden on the welfare state and take American jobs, hurting the U.S. economy, or that it is nativism directed toward all foreign groups (Nowrasteh, 2018). However, the U.S.'s history of selective immigration, favoring immigrants of European or Christian decent, suggests that the underlying motivation of opposing refugees and Mexican immigrants is the concern that they will become a threat to the safety of U.S. citizens. Racial bars to U.S. citizenship persisted until 1952; before this the definition of white was expanded to accommodate for certain European groups, including Irish and Italian Catholics and Eastern European Jews. Immigrants from non-Western cultures, specifically immigrants of Asian descent, encountered similar discrimination as Mexican immigrants and Syrian refugees are facing today, largely based on fear in response to certain events. A significant example is the imprisonment of 112,000 Japanese Americans in concentration camps in response to Pearl Harbor (Oppenheimer, D.B., Prakash, S. and Burns, R., 2016). Muslim and Mexican immigrants have faced similar explicit and targeted discrimination. For example, in 2017 the Trump Administration enacted a travel ban against all majority-Muslim countries, preventing admission into the U.S. Also in 2017, the Trump Administration revoked the Deferred Action for Childhood Arrivals program, of which 94% of recipients are Latino (Srikantiah and Sinnar, 2019). These policy actions are likely in response to stereotypes bred in response to high-profile terrorist attacks and other crimes.

Opposition towards admitting Syrian refugees could embody racial fear towards a specific group of people: those of Middle Eastern descent. In 2016, the year my data was collected, multiple terrorist attacks occurred in Europe. The Islamic State, also known as ISIS, claimed responsibility for the majority of these attacks. Due to the association of these attacks with Islam, some individuals will likely fear anyone from these majority-Muslim countries coming into the U.S., believing that terrorists may pose as refugees. This assumption is supported by the stereotype established against Muslims in the aftermath of 9/11/2001; inciting that they are against democratic, Western values. The term "Islamophobia" became popularized by the media in response to such attitudes, showing how common this prejudice has become. For example, Buncombe (2017) reports that "incidents of Islamophobia rose by 57 per cent in 2016." Based on these developments, some U.S. citizens may retain negative attitudes towards any Muslims, including refugees, entering the country, solely based on their race and ethnicity. U.S. citizens with Islamophobia likely see their admittance as a threat, and in anticipation of possible terrorist attacks, may seek extra measures of self-defense.

It could be argued that guns are not an effective means of stopping terrorist attacks, as terrorists sometimes use tactics such as suicide bombing and motor vehicles. However, the two largest terrorist attacks in 2015, the January 7th attack on the *Charlie Hebdo* offices and the November 13th attack on various locations in Paris, were largely carried out with guns (Onyanga-Omara, 2016). These events brought the gun control debate back into the news and spiked gun sales in the U.S., which reached 1.5 million sales in December 2015 (Aisch and Keller, 2016). These facts suggest there is a relationship between terrorist attacks and conversation and action surrounding guns.

Support for increased border control can derive from fear of illegal immigrants coming into the U.S. from Mexico. Similar to refugees, illegal immigrants have made national news for committing crimes. While these crimes have not occurred on as wide a scale as terrorist attacks, they have involved murders of some Americans. It is also a stereotype that these illegal immigrants funnel drugs into the U.S. All of these biases suggest that some Americans would be fearful towards illegal immigrants. Because the crimes they are associated with often involve guns, some U.S. citizens may find guns to be an assuring self-defense mechanism. Supporting easier access to concealed-carry permits could reflect this belief and fear against illegal immigrants.

The Syrian refugee crisis and the debate over illegal immigration were both controversial studies in the U.S. in 2016. Contributing to the popularity of these issues, 2016 was a presidential election year in the U.S., which suggests that policy issues, including gun control and those involving race, were more in the public eye than an average year. Border control was an issue highly debated throughout the election. Then-presidential candidate Donald Trump's rhetoric towards illegal immigrants, specifically his plan to build a wall on the U.S.-Mexican border, was particularly polarizing. For example, his immigration reform campaign platform stated, under the subheading *Make Mexico Pay For The Wall*, "Mexico's leaders have been taking advantage of the United States by using illegal immigration to export the crime and poverty in their own country" (Trump, 2015). The wall shows a measure of self-defense the president wants to enact against illegal immigrants, and this policy may have influenced individuals to pursue their own self-defense against the same group of people. Donald Trump similarly condemned the U.S.'s lack of security against terrorists. Using the slogan "Make America Safe Again," in a 2016 campaign speech he announced his plan to "suspend immigration from some of the most dangerous and volatile regions of the world that have a history of exporting terrorism" (Trump, 2016). Rhetoric such as this, especially when spread through social media, infiltrates the minds of citizens, and causes many to form an opinion before they further educate themselves on the topic. Because much of this rhetoric is negative, many Americans may have formed negative views of these groups, leading Americans to fear them.

The 2016 presidential race was also characterized by its strict party divisions. Throughout the campaign trail, political issues, including those of race and gun control, became more polarized between Democrats and Republicans. Because of these factors, ideology may be a significant determinant of people's opinions on certain issues at the time of the survey. However, there may be individuals that consider issues, such as those involving race and concealed-carry permits, independently from their party's influence. There may also be moderates that have opinions on issues that align with different parties' platforms. This disparity is where opinions on issues involving gun control could be influenced by other factors, such as attitudes toward race.

Based on my assumptions and the controversial environment in which issues regarding race and gun control are interacting, I hypothesize that having an opinion that embodies racial fear is a significant causal factor of supporting easier access to concealed-carry permits. The idea of racial fear is manifested specifically in opposing illegal immigration by advocating for increasing border security and opposing admittance of Syrian refugees. People are naturally afraid of things different from or unfamiliar to them, and owning weapons could be a way for individuals to take action against their fear of races different from their own and prevent these groups from disrupting Americans' way of life. This may be especially true if they believe that these newcomers will incite violence.

Additionally, because of the negative media coverage and politically-charged context surrounding refugees and illegal immigrants in America, I hypothesize that the relationship between general racial fear and support for easier access to permits will be weaker than those between opposition toward refugees and support for easier access to permits and support for increased border security and support for easier access to permits.

H1: The more racially fearful a respondent is, the more likely they will support easier access to concealed-carry permits.

H2: Opposing Syrian refugees will increase the likelihood of supporting easier access to concealed-carry permits.

H3: Supporting increased border security will increase the likelihood of supporting easier access to concealed-carry permits.

H4: The relationship between racial fear and supporting easier access to concealed-carry permits will be lesser in magnitude than those between opposing Syrian refugees and supporting easier access to concealed-carry permits and supporting increased border security and supporting easier access to concealed-carry permits.

Empirical Strategy
In this paper, I am interested in that which influences support for easier access to concealed-carry permits, specifically racial fear, support for increased security at the U.S.-Mexican border and opposition to Syrian refugees entering the U.S.

Data
For this analysis, I leverage nationally representative survey data from the 2016 Cooperative Congressional Election Survey (CCES). The 2016 CCES includes 64,600 responses from adult American citizens (Ansolabehere and Schaffner, 2017).

Variables of Interest
My dependent variable is whether or not individuals support easier access to concealed-carry permits. The dependent variable, then, is the response to the survey question "Make it easier for people to obtain concealed-carry permit," and was coded as 1 = "Yes" and 0 = "No".

The three main independent variables are "Racial Fear", "Increase the number of border agents on the U.S.-Mexican border," and "Admit No Refugees from Syria." I coded the variable "Racial Fear" as categorical on a scale of 1 to 5, with 1 being "Strongly Disagree" with the statement "I often find myself fearful of people of other races," and 5 being "Strongly Agree" with the same statement. "Increase the number of border agents on the U.S.-Mexican border" was measured by respondents selecting the phrase as a policy action they support, and was coded as 1 = "Yes" and 0 = "No". "Admit No Refugees from Syria" was also dichotomous and coded the same way, as 1 = "Yes" and 0 = "No".

I present summary statistics for my variables of interest in Tables 1 and 2 and Figures 1, 2, and 3 below. The raw number of respondents for each category was converted into the percentage of respondents that identified with that category, rounded to the nearest tenth. As shown below, Racial Fear strongly trends towards disagree, as for each increase on the 1 to 5 scale, the percentage of respondents in the category decreases. Opinions on admitting refugees from Syria also trends strongly in one direction, as almost double the percentage of respondents expressed support for admitting refugees than expressed opposition. Increasing border security appears to be much more divisive, as the percentage of respondents in each category is almost equal. Making it easier to obtain concealed-carry permits is also divided, as the group that opposes easier access is larger than the group that favors increased access by about 24%.

Table 1. Racial Fear Variable

Strongly Disagree	Somewhat Disagree	Neither Agree nor Disagree	Somewhat Agree	Strongly Agree
38.2%	24.2%	22.6%	12.1%	2.6%

Table 2. Yes/No Independent Variables and Dependent Variable

Variable	Responses: Yes	Responses: No
Admit No Refugees from Syria	35.9%	64.1%
Increase the number of border agents on the U.S.-Mexican border	49.3%	50.6%
Make it easier for people to obtain concealed-carry permit	37.5%	61.9%

I controlled for gender, education level, race, and political ideology.[1] Gender may have an impact on opinion toward concealed-carry permits because it is a general consensus among scholars that men are more likely to apply for permits and own handguns than women (Shapira, Jensen, and Lin, 2017, Lott 2018). Education level may also have an impact, as fewer college graduates own guns than non-graduates (Parker, Horowitz, Igielnik, Oliphant, and Brown, 2017). Because the independent variables I am testing are issues involving race, race is a necessary control. Political ideology is important to control for because border security and the refugee crisis were two important election issues in 2016, the year my data was compiled. Because liberals and conservatives overall took strong opposing stances on these issues, respondents' answers may have been influenced by their political party's stance. In a perfect world, I would control for all possible causal factors, such as if the respondent was from a Southern state and if the respondent owned a handgun at the time of the survey. However, because the survey did not ask these questions, I could not include these variables in my models, and limit controls to those previously mentioned.

Contingency Graphs for Variables of Interest

In Figures 1, 2, and 3 I display counts of responses for each independent variable disaggregated by responses to the dependent variable categories (support for increased access to permits (1) or not (0)). As shown in Figure 1, with the exception of levels 1 and 2, the proportion of respondents that support increased access to concealed-carry permits increases with each level of racial fear. In Figure 2, the proportion of respondents who support increased access to concealed-carry permits is much higher in respondents that oppose admitting refugees from Syria. Figure 3 shows that the proportion of respondents who support increased access to concealed-carry permits is greater in those who support increased border security than those who oppose it. The numeric output behind Figures 1, 2, and 3 is displayed in Appendix 1.

---

[1] Descriptive statistics for all control variables are included in Appendix 3.

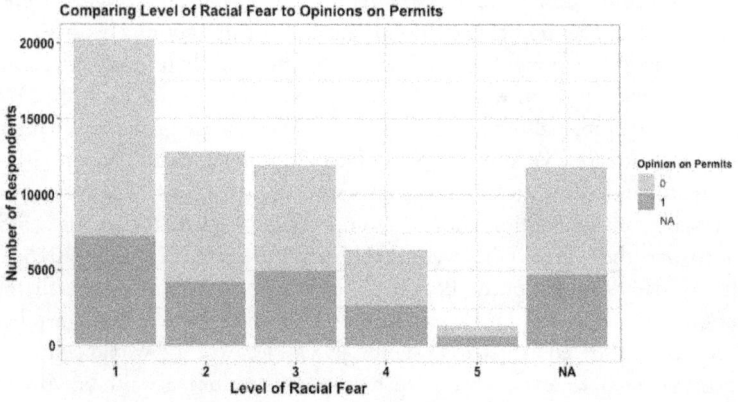

Figure 1: Comparing Level of Racial Fear to Opinions on Permits

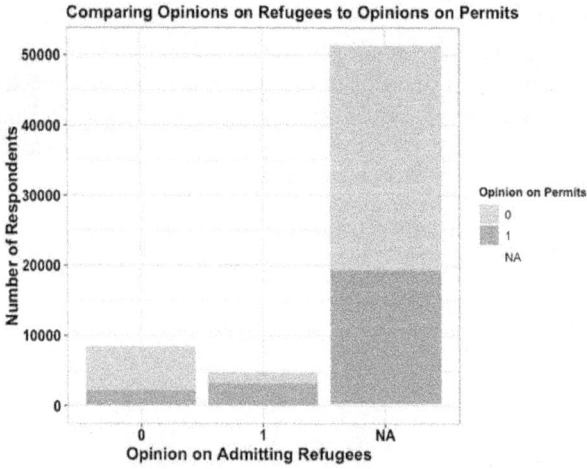

Figure 2: Comparing Opinions on Refugees to Opinions on Permits

Comparing Opinions on Increased Border Security to Opinions on Permits

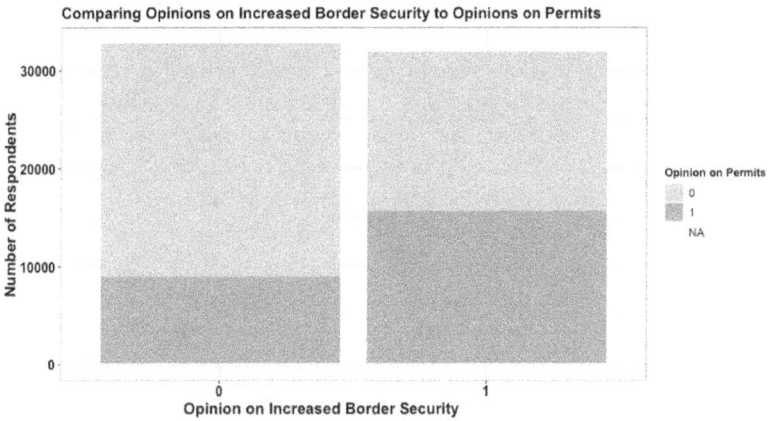

Figure 3: Comparing Opinions on Increased Border Security to Opinions on Permints

Modeling Strategy

To test my hypotheses, given that my dependent variable is binary, I estimate a series of logistic regressions. A logistic regression models the probability that a dependent variable will take on a value of 1, relative to the baseline of 0. In my context, I am interested in the probability that support for a particular policy action or admitting a certain amount of racial fear will increase the likelihood of supporting easier access to permits. I fit four regressions, regressing the dependent variable on each of my independent variables of interest individually (with controls), and then on all independent variables. I present these results in Table 3 below.

Results

I turn now to explore the effects of my independent variables of interest, level of racial fear, opinion towards border security at the U.S.-Mexican border and opinion towards admitting Syrian refugees into the U.S., on my dependent variable, opinion towards easier access to concealed-carry permits. I present the results in Table 3.

Looking at the fourth (4) column in Table 3, which reports results from the fully specified model, the most prominent finding is that opposing admittance of Syrian refugees and supporting increased border security are positive and significant predictors for supporting increased access to concealed-carry permits. Substantively, this means that supporting increasing border security as a policy action makes a respondent more likely to support easier access to concealed-carry permits. Similarly, if a respondent opposes admittance of Syrian refugees, then they are more likely to support easier access to concealed-carry permits. Racial fear has a slightly negative and no significant effect on opinion towards easier access to concealed-carry permits. The results are in line with expectations, as racial fear is likely attenuated by social desirability bias, while the proxies for racial fear (border security support and refugee opposition) are strong predictors for preferring increased access to concealed-carry permits.[2]

Table 3. The Effect of Racial Fear on Support for Increased Access to Concealed-Carry Permits

	(1)	(2)	(3)	(4)
Racial Fear	0.055***			−0.015
	(0.009)			(0.020)
Opposed Admit Refugees		1.149***		0.997***
		(0.046)		(0.050)
Support Increased Border Security			0.554***	0.506***
			(0.019)	(0.053)
Female	−0.565***	−0.551***	−0.542***	−0.534***
	(0.021)	(0.043)	(0.019)	(0.045)
Race	0.015*	0.102***	0.012	0.102***
	(0.008)	(0.018)	(0.007)	(0.018)
Education	−0.081***	−0.052***	−0.073***	−0.042***
	(0.007)	(0.015)	(0.006)	(0.016)
Political Ideology	0.823***	0.851***	0.662***	0.815***
	(0.011)	(0.025)	(0.010)	(0.026)
Constant	−2.631***	−3.248***	−2.316***	−3.420***
	(0.054)	(0.112)	(0.044)	(0.123)
N	49,134	12,647	59,471	12,159
log likelihood	−28,108.330	−6,499.005	−34,600.700	−6,125.213
AIC	56,228.650	13,010.010	69,213.400	12,266.420

Notes:
[1] Dependent variable: Support Increased Access to Concealed-Carry Permits (1=yes; 0=no);
[2] Standard errors in parentheses;
[3] Significance levels: ∗ : 10% ∗∗ : 5% ∗∗∗ : 1%

[2] To verify the robustness of all models, I calculate and compare Akaike Information Criterion (AIC) and Bayesian Information Criterion (BIC) statistics. Across all comparisons, where lower AIC and BIC suggest a better fit and less information loss, the full model including all of the variables and controls, was the best fitting model to the data. These tests are included in Appendix 2 for AIC and BIC, respectively.

Predicted Probabilities

While the coefficients in Table 3 are valuable for explaining direction and significance of the model effects, a more intuitive look at these results is through inspecting predicted probabilities. Specifically, I calculate out of sample predicted probabilities for my two significant independent variables, opposition towards admitting Syrian refugees and support for increased border security, and display them below in Figures 4 and 5. Predicted probabilities represent the probability of supporting greater access to concealed-carry permits as a function of the key independent variables of interest, over the range of some other variable, which in my case is political ideology, ranging from 1 to 5, with 1 being "Very liberal" and 5 being "Very conservative". Ideology is displayed on the x-axis of Figures 4 and 5. The predicted probability of a respondent supporting increased access to concealed-carry permits is displayed on the y-axis, ranging from 0 to 100%. The red line in both graphs represents respondents who disagree with the policy action being proposed. In Figure 4, the policy action is opposing refugee admittance. In Figure 5, the policy action is increasing border security. In both graphs the blue line represents respondents that support the respective policy action. The 95% confidence intervals for the predictions are represented by the gray shading surrounding the lines. These graphs display the effect of the independent variables on the dependent variable at each level of ideology, allowing us to isolate the effects of ideology from the effects of the independent variables.

In Figure 4, the positive slopes show that as ideology becomes more conservative, the probability of supporting increased access to concealed-carry permits increases. While this was expected, within ideology levels there is a significant difference in the probability of supporting increased access to concealed-carry between those who support admittance of refugees and oppose admittance of refugees. Among those who support refugee admittance, the most liberal have about a 5% probability of supporting increased access to concealed-carry permits, compared to a probability of 15% among the most liberal who oppose refugee admittance, resulting in an estimated 10% difference in probability between groups. On the other side of the ideological spectrum, "very conservative," those who support refugee admittance have about an 63% probability of supporting increased access to concealed-carry permits. Those who are very conservative but oppose refugee admittance have about an 85% probability of supporting increased access to concealed-carry permits, resulting in an estimated 22% difference in probability between groups.

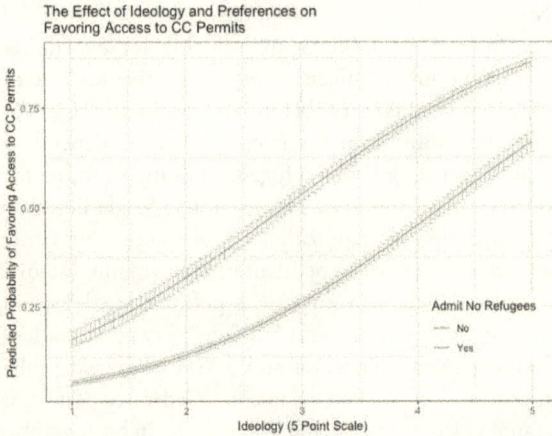

The Effect of Ideology and Preferences on Favoring Access to CC Permits

Figure 4: Predicted Probabilities of Favoring Increased Access to Concealed-Carry Permits According to Opinion on Refugee Admittance

Similar to Figure 4, Figure 5 shows that the more conservative a respondent is, the more likely they will support increased access to concealed-carry permits. However, when ideology is held constant there is a significant difference in the probability of supporting increased access to concealed-carry between those who support increased border security and those who oppose it. Among the most liberal respondents, those who do not support increased border security have about a 5% probability of supporting increased access to concealed-carry permits. This is compared to about a 15% probability among the most liberal that do support increased border security, resulting in an estimated 10% difference. Among the most conservative respondents there is not as large of a difference between groups compared to when based on opinion towards refugee admittance, but the results are still significant. Those who do not support increasing border security have about a 60% probability of supporting increased access to concealed-carry permits, while those who support increasing border security have slightly above a 70% probability of supporting increased access to concealed-carry permits, an estimated 10% difference.

The Effect of Ideology and Preferences on
Favoring Access to CC Permits

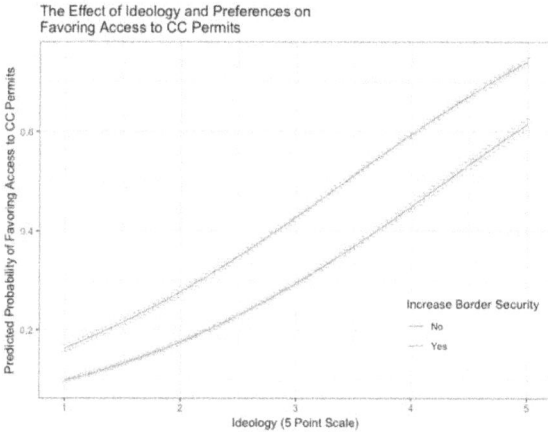

Figure 5: Predicted Probabilities of Favoring Increased Access to Concealed-Carry Permits
According to Opinion on Increased Border Security

In sum, the predicted probabilities in Figures 4 and 5 show that while ideology influences attitudes towards increased access to concealed-carry permits, opinions towards refugee admittance and increased border security also maintain high significance in determining opinion towards concealed-carry permits. Regardless of ideology, a respondent who opposes refugee admittance is more likely to support increased access to concealed-carry permits. Likewise, a respondent who supports increased border security is more likely to support increased access to concealed-carry permits.

Odds Ratios

To view the findings in a different light, I now explore odds ratios for each significant independent variable of interest. Odds ratios are used to measure the association between two variables; predicting the odds that a certain outcome will occur with the exposure of a certain variable. In this context, odds ratios predict the likelihood a respondent will support increased access to concealed-carry permits at the exposure of opposing refugee admittance and supporting increased border security. I only calculated odds ratios for the fourth model, as it is fully specified. The odds ratios are displayed in Table 4, along with the 95% confidence intervals for each variable.

Table 4. Odds Ratios

	Odds Ratio	2.5%	97.5%
(Intercept)	0.033	0.026	0.042
Racial Fear	0.985	0.947	1.025
Opposed Admit Refugees	2.709	2.454	2.991
Support Increased Border Security	1.659	1.496	1.839
Female	0.586	0.537	0.640
Race	1.108	1.068	1.148
Education	0.959	0.929	0.989
Political ideology	2.258	2.146	2.378

In line with findings to this point, opposes refugee admittance has an odds ratio of 2.709, meaning that a respondent who supports admitting refugees into the U.S. is 170.9% more likely to support increased access to permits. Supporting increased border security has an odds ratio of 1.659, meaning that there is a 65.9% increase in the likelihood that a respondent who supports increasing border security will also support easier access to permits. These outcomes are consistent with my hypotheses, suggesting that opposing admittance of Syrian refugees is positively related to supporting easier access to permits, and supporting increased border security is positively related to supporting increased access to permits.

Conclusion
The purpose of this paper was to find if racial fear determines attitudes towards gun control. The motivation behind exploring this relationship was the resurgence of racial issues in the U.S. and the simultaneous increase in gun-related deaths. Race was a factor in many of these deaths, such as in the shooting of unarmed minorities. By exploring this relationship, we can better understand the public's motive behind certain policies, which would allow policymakers to target certain behaviors if they want to enact change.

In line with expectations, I found that supporting increased border security and opposing refugee admittance had a positive and significant effect on supporting increased access to concealed-carry permits. A respondent that supports increased border security is more likely to support increased access to concealed-carry permits, as is a respondent who opposes Syrian refugees coming into the U.S. Level of racial fear was found to have an insignificant and negative effect, possibly due to social desirability bias. These results support my theory that racial fear influences supporting increased gun control. Individuals who fear other races and see them as a threat want a way to defend themselves, and concealed-carry permits are the most direct way to self-defense in public. To reinforce my findings, I calculated predicted probabilities for my two significant independent variables of interest, support for increased border security and opposition towards admitting Syrian refugees, while controlling specifically for ideology. The results echoed the regression: at all levels of ideology, respondents who are more likely to support increased border security or oppose Syrian refugee admittance are more likely to support increased access to concealed-carry permits.

Though thorough, this research is still limited. Most notably, I only looked at cross sectional data at a moment in time, in the midst of a hyper-polarized political climate. Future studies could test these expectations with survey data from other years and even other countries. Further, a topic for future discussion could be how to dispel the negative bias surrounding these groups. Based on this research, we know that racial bias exists and is affecting opinions towards other areas of policy. By aiming to reduce bias, we could enact policy creation that would promote cooperation and peace throughout the U.S.

References

Ansolabehere, Stephen, and Brian F. Schaffner. 2017. "CCES Common Content, 2016." *Harvard Dataverse*. https://doi.org/10.7910/DVN/GDF6Z0.

Aisch, Gregor, and Josh Keller. 2016. "What Happens After Calls for New Gun Restrictions? Sales Go Up." *The New York Times*, June 13. https://www.nytimes.com/interactive/2015/12/10/us/gun-sales-terrorism-obama-restrictions.html.

Banks, Antoine J. and Heather M. Hicks. 2015. "Fear and Implicit Racism: Whites' Support for Voter ID Laws." *Political Psychology* 37(5): 641 – 658.

Bassett, Jonathan F. and Jennifer N. Connelly. 2011. "Terror Management and Reactions to Undocumented Immigrants: Mortality Salience Increases Aversion to Culturally Dissimilar Others." *Journal of Social Psychology* 151(2): 117-120.

Berinsky, Adam. 2004. *Silent Voices*. Princeton, New Jersey: Princeton University Press.

Bhatia, Amit A. 2015. "Perspectives, Attitudes and Practices of American Evangelicals towards Muslims in the U.S." PhD diss. Trinity Evangelical Divinity School.

Bhatia, Rukmani. 2019. "Guns, Lies, and Fear: Exposing the NRA's Messaging Playbook." *Center for American Progress*. https://www.americanprogress.org/issues/guns-crime/reports/2019/04/24/468951/guns-lies-fear/.

Bruneau, Emile, Nour Kteily, and Lasse Laustsen. 2017. "The Unique Effects of Blatant Dehumanization on Attitudes and Behavior towards Muslim Refugees during the European 'Refugee Crisis' across Four Countries." *European Journal of Social Psychology* 48(5): 645-662.

Buncombe, Andrew. 2017. "Islamophobia Even Worse under Trump Than after 9/11 Attacks, Says Top Muslim Activist." *The Independent*, December 27. https://www.independent.co.uk/news/world/americas/us-politics/trump-islam-muslim-islamophobia-worse-911-says-leader-a8113686.html.

Liqun Cao, Francis T. Cullen, and Bruce G. Link. 2006. "The Social Determinants of Gun Ownership: Self-Protection in an Urban Environment." *Criminology* 35(4): 629-650.

Cramer, Clayton E. 1994. "The Racist Roots of Gun Control." *The Kansas Journal of Law & Public Policy* 4(2): 17-25.

Culotta, Elizabeth. 2012. "Roots of Racism." *Science*, 336(6083): 825-827.

Dawson, Jessica. 2019. "Shall not be infringed: how the NRA used religious language to transform the meaning of the Second Amendment." *Palgrave Communication* 5(58): 1- 13.

Disha, Ilir, James C. Cavendish, and Ryan D. King. 2011. "Historical Events and Spaces of Hate: Hate Crimes against Arabs and Muslims in Post-9/11 America." *Social Problems* 58(1): 21-46.

Fadda-Conrey, Carol. 2011. "Arab American Citizenship in Crisis: Destabilizing Representations of Arabs and Muslims in the US after 9/11." *MFS Modern Fiction Studies,* 57(3): 532-555.

Filindra, Alexandra, and Noah J. Kaplan. 2016. "Racial resentment and Whites' Gun Policy Preferences in Contemporary America." *Political Behavior* 38(2): 255-275.

Gramlich, John. 2019. "How Americans See Illegal Immigration, the Border Wall and Political Compromise." *Pew Research Center.* https://www.pewresearch.org/fact-tank/2019/01/16/how-americans-see-illegal-immigration-the-border-wall-and-political-compromise/.

Hauser, Will, and Gary Kleck. 2013. "Guns and Fear: A One-Way Street?" *Crime & Delinquency* 59(2): 271-291.

Igielnik, Ruth, and Anna Brown. 2017. "Key takeaways on Americans' View of Guns and Gun Ownership." *Pew Research Center,* June 22. https://www.pewresearch.org/fact-tank/2017/06/22/key-takeaways-on-americans-views-of-guns-and-gun-ownership/.

Jeffrey, Courtland. 2018. "Mass Shootings in the U.S.: 346 Mass Shootings Occurred in 2017." *ABC 15 Arizona,* February 14. https://www.abc15.com/news/data/mass-shootings-in-the-u-s-over-270-mass-shootings-have-occurred-in-2017.

Kaplan, Jeffrey. 2007. "Islamophobia in America? September 11 and Islamophobic Hate Crime." *Terrorism and Political Violence* 18(1): 1-33.

Lott, John R. 2018. "Concealed Carry Permit Holders across the United States: 2018." *SSRN.* https://ssrn.com/abstract=3233904.

McDowall, David, and Colin Loftin. 1983. "Collective Security and the Demand for Legal Handguns." *American Journal of Sociology* 88(6): 1146-1161.

Mangum, Maurice, and Ray Block Jr. 2018. "Social Identity Theory and Public Opinion towards Immigration." *Social Sciences* 7(3): 1-16.

Nowrasteh, Alex. 2018. "The 14 Most Common Arguments against Immigration and Why They're Wrong." *Cato Institute*, May 2. https://www.cato.org/blog/14-most-common-arguments-against-immigration-why-theyre-wrong.

O'Brien, Kerry, Walter Forrest, Dermot Lynott, and Michael Daly. 2013. "Racism, Gun Ownership and Gun Control: Biased Attitudes in US Whites May Influence Policy Decisions." *PLoS ONE*, 8(10): e77552.

Ogan, Christine, Lars Willnat, Rosemary Pennington, and Manaf Bashir. 2014. "The Rise of Anti-Muslim Prejudice: Media and Islamophobia in Europe and the United States." *International Communication Gazette* 76(1): 27–46.

Onyanga-Omara, Jane. 2016. "Timeline: Terror attacks in Europe." *USA Today*, March 22.

Oppenheimer, David B., Swati Prakash, and Rachel Burns. 2016. "Playing the Trump Card: The Enduring Legacy of Racism in Immigration Law." *Berkeley La Raza Law Journal* 26(1): 1-45.

Parker, Kim, Juliana Horowitz, Ruth Igielnik, Baxter Oliphant, and Anna Brown. 2017. "America's Complex Relationship with Guns." *Pew Research Center*. https://www.pewsocialtrends.org/wp-content/uploads/sites/3/2017/06/Guns-Report-FOR-WEBSITE-PDF-6-21.pdf.

Pearson, Matthew R. 2010. "How "Undocumented Workers" and "Illegal Aliens" Affect Prejudice toward Muslim Immigrants." *Social Influence* 5(2): 118-132.

Pehrson, Samuel, Rupert Brown, and Hanna Zagefka. 2009. "When Does National Identification Lead to the Rejection of Immigrants? Cross-sectional and Longitudinal Evidence for the Role of Essentialist In-group Definitions." *British Journal of Social Psychology* 48(1): 61-76.

Pierre, Joseph M. 2019. "The Psychology of Guns: Risk, Fear, and Motivated Reasoning." *Palgrave Communication* 5(159): 1-7.

Rabrenovic, Gordana. 2007. "When Hate Comes to Town: Community Response to Violence Against Immigrants." *American Behavioral Scientist* 51(2): 349-360.

Rana, Junaid. 2007. "The Story of Islamophobia." *Souls* 9(2): 148-161.

Rhodan, Maya. 2017. "Gun-Related Deaths in America Keep Going Up." *Time Magazine*, November 6.

Romero, Luis, and Zarrugh, Amina. 2018. "Islamophobia and the Making of Latinos/as into Terrorist Threats." *Ethnic and Racial Studies* 41(12): 2235-2254.

Shapira, Harel, Katherine Jensen, and Ken-Hou Lin. 2017. "Trends and Patterns of Concealed Handgun License Applications: A Multistate Analysis." *Social Currents* 5(1): 3-14.

Smith, Samantha. 2017. "Young People Less Likely to View Iraqi, Syrian Refugees as Major Threat to U.S." *Pew Research Center.* https://www.pewresearch.org/fact-tank/2017/02/03/young-people-less-likely-to-view-iraqi-syrian-refugees-as-major-threat-to-u-s/.

Srikantiah, Jayashri, and Shirin Sinnar. 2019. "White Nationalism as Immigration Policy." *Stanford Law Review* 71(6).

Swaine, Jon, Oliver Laughland, Jamiles Lartey, and Ciara McCarthy. 2015. "Young Black Men Killed by US Police at Highest Rate in Year of 1,134 Deaths." *The Guardian*, December 31.

Trump, Donald. 2015. "Immigration Reform That Will Make America Great Again." https://assets.donaldjtrump.com/Immigration-Reform-Trump.pdf.

Trump, Donald. 2016. "Donald Trump's Speech on Fighting Terrorism." *Politico*, August 15. https://www.politico.com/story/2016/08/donald-trump-terrorism-speech-227025.

Waugaman, Elisabeth. 2016. "Understanding America's Obsession with Guns: How Did We Get Where We Are?" *Psychoanalytic Inquiry* 36(6): 440-453.

Willingham, AJ, and Ahmed Saeed. 2017. "Mass shootings in America are a serious problem – and these 9 charts show just why." *CNN*, November 6. https://www.cnn.com/2016/06/13/health/mass-shootings-in-america-in-charts-and-graphs-trnd/index.html.

Zaal, Mayida. 2012. "Islamophobia in Classrooms, Media, and Politics." *Journal of Adolescent and Adult Literacy* 55(6): 555-558.

Appendices

Appendix 1: Cross-Tabs for Variables of Interest

Table A1. Comparing Level of Racial Fear to Opinions on Permits

	Racial Fear				
Pro Permit	1	2	3	4	5
0	12,962	8,563	7,032	3,671	674
1	7,173	4,196	4,837	2,678	680

Table A2. Comparing Opposition Toward Refugees to Opinions on Permits

	Admit No Refugees	
Pro Permit	0	1
0	3,402	4,586
1	1,236	3,937

Table A3. Comparing Supporting Border Security to Opinions on Permits

	Increase border security	
Pro Permit	0	1
0	23,784	16,198
1	8,753	15,488

Appendix 2: Model Fit Checks

Table B1. Akaike Information Criterion (AIC) and Bayesian Information Criterion (BIC)

Model	AIC	BIC
Full	12266.43	12325.67
Racial fear	56228.65	56281.47
Increase border security	69213.4	69267.36
Admit no refugees	13010.01	13054.68

Appendix 3: Summary Statistics for Control Variables

Table C1. Gender Statistics

Male	Female
29,531	35,069

Table C2. Education Level

No High School	High School Graduate	Some College	Two-year College	Four-year College	Post-grad degree
1,971	16,381	15,685	7,169	14,884	8,510

Table C3. Race

White	Black	Hispanic	Asian	Native American	Middle Eastern	Mixed	Other
46,289	7,926	5,238	2,278	522	135	1,452	760

Table C4. Ideology

Very Liberal	Liberal	Moderate	Conservative	Very Conservative
5,827	12,555	22,040	14,351	5,042

www.ingramcontent.com/pod-product-compliance
Lightning Source LLC
Chambersburg PA
CBHW022341280326
41934CB00006B/728